LITERARY TRANSLATION
& POETRY

LITERARY TRANSLATION
& POETRY

UEA MA
Creative Writing Anthologies
2024

LITERARY TRANSLATION

KARI DICKSON	Foreword	VII
CECILIA ROSSI	Introduction	IX
EILEEN CRAIGIE	Wessi	2
M. JOSÉ GALEANO	The Universe is Homeland	8
ANNIE GRANGER	In the Boat	12
MEGAN HARVEY	Ironwood	18
JON RUSSELL HERRING	The Haven	26
PARIS JONCHIER-LITWACK	That Man's Mother	32
ELIZABETH LUTZ	Maybe It Matters To You	38
CAITLIN MCKIE	Be My Baby	48
ANA SOPHIA PLATT	The Ghosts of Frost Island	52
CHRIS SALPINGIDIS	Prologos, Epeisodia A & B, Exodos	58
	Acknowledgements	162

POETRY

JOELLE TAYLOR	Foreword	XI
HOLLY CORFIELD CARR	Introduction	XIII
BADRIYA ABDULLAH		66
DANA COLLLINS		72
SARAH HULME		78
MEIER SMITH		82
PAUL MARTELL		88
TABITHA BENNETT		92
MICHAEL ATHEY		98
EDEN CHICKEN		104
MIDORI TAKAHASHI		112
LUCY CUNDILL		118
NAOISE GALE		128
DANIEL NORTHOVER		134
EMMA BROWN		140
FLORA BEAGLEY		146
MISHAL AHMAD		154
Acknowledgements		163

KARI DICKSON
Literary Translation Foreword

Congratulations to you all!

What a gift this anthology is. You have a published translation in your hand. I still remember the thrill of seeing my name in print for the first time. Translated by. This may or may not be your first published translation, but I hope it will be one of many, many more.

People often ask me if translation is not a lonely profession. No, I reply. Solitary, yes, for a lot of the time. But never lonely. I am constantly in the company of the characters in the book I'm translating; I am often in contact with the author; when I'm stuck, I reach out to friends and colleagues, from all languages. From all over the world. Perhaps because we do spend so much time on our own, translators are some of the most generous, kind and interesting people I know. Perhaps because it is still quite a niche profession, gatherings of translators are always joyous occasions when we can nerd out and talk about the tiniest details, share news and industry gossip. But sometimes, being surrounded by translators chatting about this book and that contract, and this contact and that festival, it is all too easy to fall victim to imposter syndrome. But if you dare to confess to it, you'll discover that we all feel the same. Perhaps because it is still such a hard and precarious profession – we still have to negotiate each contract, sit up all night to meet deadlines, have our translation choices questioned by authors, editors and critics, see books we love and have worked to promote passed on to other translators – it is important to have a strong support network.

I'm also often asked if you need to have an MA to become a literary translator, and the answer is no, you don't. But it's a kind of shortcut.

You now have a solid basis for building that network.

When I did my MA in translation thirty years ago, MALT was in its infancy and the BCLT had been going for about five years. I was totally unaware of their existence. How I wish I'd known about them then.

I started out as an inhouse translator at the central bank of Norway and then carried on as a freelance translator. My journey as a literary translator began when I moved back to the UK in 2001. I remember feeling utterly bewildered when I attended my first London Book Fair. I knew no one, had no idea about how to set about it, and as it was before the Literary Translation Centre was established, there was no natural place to meet other translators. But I was fortunate enough to meet someone who had done the MA in literary translation at UEA. And I heard about

BCLT for the first time. It was a turning point. Here were people who generously shared their experience and gave me a kind of dot-to-dot map for how to navigate the literary translation business in the UK. And when I attended my first BCLT summer school as a workshop leader, my world expanded.

Having recently been one of the BCLT translators in residence, I've had the pleasure of meeting many of you, attending various workshops, having access to your reading lists, study materials and research seminars. I can see that in this year, you have gained much of the knowledge that it took me years to acquire. Theory, practice and business. It really is a fantastic and unique course.

Thanks to the generosity and great efforts of various individuals working both with and in BCLT, MALT and the Translators Association, literary translation has become so much more visible in the UK. The BCLT and MALT have gone from strength to strength and gained an international reputation for quality. And on more than one occasion, publishers have told me that when they are introduced to a new translator, they are always reassured if that person has links to BCLT and MALT.

As MALT graduates, you have the best possible starting point to embark on your own journeys into translation. To live it and then share your experience with others.

Three cheers for MALT, three cheers for BCLT!

And once again, congratulations.

Kari Dickson, 2024

CECILIA ROSSI
Literary Translation Introduction

Introducing Eileen, María José, Annie, Megan, Jon, Paris, Elizabeth, Caitlin, Ana Sophia, and Chris

> Versuchen, die Fragen selbst liebzuhaben (Rilke wrote):
> most literally, try to love the questions themselves,
> but the words I have in my head are:
> learn to love the questions themselves. Like locked
> doors or books written in a foreign language.
>
> Because difficulty
> requires time,
> requires previous reading experience,
> requires attention.
>
> For example, when translating a text, I make notes
> around words, based on my own experience.
> And the word which stands out the most to me
> (is) the path I am most drawn to.
>
> (And) on naming the drafts –
> Heartwood, Sapwood, Roots, Photosynthesis –
> I continue the metaphor of the woman becoming a tree:
> Within (her) anatomy, the source text
> would be the pith at the very centre.
>
> (And yet), to reach a publication-ready text,
> (one) is compelled to hide the traces of its production.
> How to make them visible – the sailing ship is not painted
> on the sea in what will eventually be published
> but it moves around and under (what is) presented here:

Phrasal congruity: how the musical can
not only compliment but also elevate
the textual (so we can) hear the breath
of the text, the weight of its words,
in both source and target.

I set all these thoughts
and associations down
in my translation notebook:
I don't think that anything is irrelevant
during the translation process.

(This) gave me a sense of authority.
As though pulling on one small thread such as this
made it far easier to unweave the whole tapestry:
my project has been a process of exploration,
liberation, and realisation.

(Of the) distinctive demands of spoken language.
(We) need to consider not only the semantic accuracy
but also the phonetic and cultural authenticity
that will resonate with the listeners.

The second version begins, addresses
its imagery – "still like a twilit tree" –
conveys suggests carries
connotations - it aligns with the need
to convey deep emotional states.

JOELLE TAYLOR
Poetry Foreword

'No one sleeps in this room without the dream of a common language'
—Adrienne Rich, The Dream of a Common Language

There is a sense in which all poetry is an act of translation.

I began this adventure in thinking and form as a teenager, compelled by a need to translate personal injustice into a scream that rhymed. Without a guide to help me decipher the foreign language of poetry, my translations were brutal and vague, leading perhaps more to a lack of understanding than to the pure act of communication that poetry can be. It took years of reading, considering, failing, and running hard into the brick walls of books before I finally began to understand what poetry was saying to me. Listen, it said. I am speaking.

Poetry is a language that lives beneath the skin. It knows our heart better than we do. It talks about us when we leave the room. It is the constant interpreter, a narrator that will walk beside you throughout your fresh lives. In the same way that Robert Feynman said *'if you understand quantum mechanics then you don't understand quantum mechanics'* I would suggest the same is true of poetry. It defies itself. Once named it stops being. As loud, as garrulous, as insistent as it can be, poetry is a quiet language. It is the language of the revolutionary and the radical, the quiet thinkers scratching new worlds on the walls of the bedsits. It is what is almost said.

You are each at the beginning of an extraordinary journey that if walked well will lead you back to yourselves. Ahead of you, everything is unwritten. The page has no footsteps punctuating it yet, but it knows you are coming. You each have a sincere duty to this strange language, this compulsion to create small worlds, have spent your years in study and dream to arrive at this moment. These are the magical moments, these spaces between, this inheld breath. And to become a poet, or an author, is to Become, to step into strange skins. But it is crucial to keep close throughout the understanding that poetry is not just an art but a responsibility. This book is alive with responsibility and duty, it seeks the small stories that say vast things, it worries at ideas as if they are seeds stuck between teeth. Pluck out the seeds and plant them. Watch them grow. Each their fruit.

There are works in this book that navigate body, and mouth, and language, and death, and desire, and exile, that think around the family, and grief, and the loss of origin. It is a compendium of bridge building remembering that, to paraphrase Roger Robinson, poems are small empathy machines. The book asks what a leaf thinks when it falls, reminds us that every poem is a Trojan horse, that it time travels, that it is atemporal.

It is an honour to be asked to write this Foreword to the anthology and a genuine thrill to welcome each of you into this odd little life. I want to leave you with one thought. For most of my life I have thought that poetry is the answer, only to discover – with a certain joy – that it is not. Poetry is the question.

Joelle Taylor, 2024

HOLLY CORFIELD CARR
Poetry Introduction

William Carlos Williams' famous definition of a poem as "a small (or large) machine made out of words" follows his (perhaps a little less famous) definition of a machine: "There's nothing sentimental about a machine". Side by side, the two definitions get into something of a logical argument which leads us to the conclusion that a poem must be largely (or smally) unsentimental. For Williams, "unsentimental" means something like *sufficient*, an unsentimental poem being precisely no more nor less than what it needs to be to get to work. He goes on to use the word "pruned", which should position the poet as a gardener, the poem as a plant cut back, the pair of them dreaming of next year's growth but, coming from a poet mostly famous for plums, "pruned" makes it sound like the poem might be a bit dehydrated. If a poem works, does it really have to be so *dry*? Is there such a machine that works well *wetly*?

The workshop in which the poets in these pages met and made their poems has been remarkable for its fearlessness as well as its sense of fun and these sorts of daft and difficult questions were common, the air of the classroom crackling with the ingenuity of the poets' answers. Of course, in any workshop, as we tilt our heads over the poem laid out on the table, sharing our tools to work out whether it is the particular torque of a line break or the crossed wires of a mixed metaphor in need of adjustment, we often find ourselves talking about whether a poem *works* as if it's a mini fridge (with or without plums for breakfast).

In this year's workshop, though, this idea of what a poem might need to get it working was almost as alchemical as it was mechanical. The poets' attention tuned to feeling as much as to function. Each poet I taught this year found a different way to teach me that if the poem is a machine at all, it seems to share the delicate, delicious machinery of the plum, from the ease of a bruise to the compost. The poets' openness to the idea that it might be necessary for a poem to be able to break down for it to work at all led to exhilarating experiments with languages that leaked into one another, forms that flooded the page or punctuation that landed like a glance of rain and caused me, their astonished reader, to look up to see the sky changing.

Adrienne Rich suggests that, like stones which dry to a dullness when lifted from the stream, it is the "wash of poetry" that keeps those words shining. In the confluence of language and life, thinking and feeling, the workshop immerses us in that wild wash, and I hope you might enjoy reading these poems which were made, unmade and made new in that place, still gleaming.

Holly Corfield Carr

LITERARY TRANSLATION

EILEEN CRAIGIE

Eileen is a writer, translator and editor. She translates from German to English and writes her own fiction, experimenting with language and form. A short story of hers was highly commended by the HISSAC prize. She lives in Norwich, UK.

eileencraigie@gmail.com

Wessi

An abridged translation from German of Finn-Ole Heinrich's 'Wessi', published as part of his collection *Gestern war auch schon ein Tag* (2009).

I don't like being with Wessi. He smells strange. The smell reminds me of decay, of dead animals, of dead birds on the roadside in summer. It's winter now. Two weeks to Christmas Eve. You wouldn't know it here. In the West, in Kaufland, you would: there it's all chocolate Santa Clauses, stollen and glühwein, all red and green and twinkling. But out here? Just the rush of the autobahn, the screech of circular saws, and the television. That's the only thing that feels like home. On television of course it's Christmas too.

I've been working in construction for the past six years. I have my own caravan. Others pay for a container. Six euros fifty per day. But you can bring your own vehicle if you have one. More space, more quiet. Not the constant coughing through the thin metal walls, not the restless shuffling, not the smells, not the rubbish.

I stand in the kitchen with Wessi, we smoke. I don't like being here, but Wessi says he has a job for me: 'I'm going to make you an offer you can't refuse.'
'Not interested, I'm wrecked, I want to go to bed.' I don't particularly like Wessi. And out here you don't care about making friends.
Construction work is solitary. The day doesn't have to be made any longer. Life in the containers is to be endured. That's all: get on, get through. It's about making the time between Monday morning and Friday afternoon as monotonous as possible, then time becomes imperceptible and slips by. Life is something you do at weekends or on holiday. That's why we're going to America. Sylvia and I, two weeks. That's why I'm standing here and listening to Wessi's spiel, maybe I can top up the holiday fund. I save everything for Sylvia. Nine days more of work, then straight to the airport. Wessi holds out a beer. I don't want to stand here and drink with him, but a beer's a beer and a gift's a gift, so I take it. I sit down.
'No nonsense, Wessi, got it? I don't have time.'
He sits down and shakes his head and says: 'Listen up, Ändi,' as if we're pals.
I say: 'An-dre-as.'
He lifts his head and changes his voice: 'Herr Brauner, I require your assistance. For two hours' work. Tonight.'
'Doing what?'
'Standing around, pretending to be a soldier.'
'Pretending to be a soldier?'
'Yep, dog on leash, gun in hand, keeping an eye out.'

'I can do that.'

'I know. That's why I'm asking you.'

'Is it illegal?'

At that Wessi starts laughing and looks at me: 'What do you think I'm doing at night in the woods with soldiers? Baking plätzchen for Christmas?'

Some people are scared shitless of retirement. They don't know what to do with themselves. That's what they're scared of, the boredom. This is my advantage. I spend so much time thinking about what I'd rather be doing, so when I'm retired I'll never be bored. This is my philosophy: better to have it really good and really bad, rather than the mush that most people have. My life has to be exceptional, I want to experience something exceptional. And the quickest way for me to earn money for such a life is in construction.

Every weekend we do something exceptional. And Sylvia comes along. She totally gets it, she wants the most out of life, she knows that I'm working here for us, for our future together. Sylvia, who I love, because she wears short skirts and often nothing underneath and because she texts me every night and sometimes cooks meals for my week in the caravan.

Wessi taps his cigarette and explains that he breeds dogs in a kennel in the woods. Pit bulls, fighting dogs. He says he breeds and trains them and when they're ready he sells them. And tonight he's selling three animals to one buyer, that's why he needs a second man. Also, it's a new customer, a Nazi he doesn't know.

One hundred and fifty, cash.

'Just stand there, gun in hand and keep an eye out,' he repeats, like I'm stupid. He gives me a black bomber jacket and a black hat.

'But that's ridiculous,' I say, before pulling on both.

'Now let's go,' he says and we walk a while through the stretch of wood, which begins just a few metres back from the containers. I'm not scared. Beyond the wood, we approach a building.

He shows me the dogs. There are about twenty, all in small crates. Young, ferocious, they bark and bite at the wire when you walk past. It stinks like Wessi's container, cloying, rotten, like dog shit. The smell of the West.

'I train the dogs,' Wessi says. 'You can't just send them into the ring. They've got to have a couple of fights, otherwise they don't stand a chance. That's why I have Bella, for training.'

Wessi holds a cigarette out to me. 'In half an hour the Nazis are coming,' he says and gives me a light.

Wessi scoops half a sack of dry food and three tins of wet food into a bucket and then adds a large bottle of energy drink and grins: 'Special recipe.' The dogs gulp down the lot greedily.

I get the ugliest dog of all. A white bulldog, scarred, bitten, covered in wounds and scabs. Wessi gives me the leash, a chain.

'Bella,' says Wessi, who either has no taste or is actually pretty funny. Funny in a Western-kind-of-way which I don't get. Why is Wessi called Wessi anyway? Do I actually know where he's from? It could just be his name. Florian Wessi or Jürgen Wessels or something like that. In any case he acts like a Westerner.

'It's loaded, careful,' says Wessi and holds out the gun. I take it. I could shoot Bella on the spot and kill her, if I wanted. Or Wessi. Or the Nazi.

'How much do you sell them for?'

We load the dogs into the rusty Lada, there's hardly space but it'll do, it's not far to the meeting point. Once there, we get out and wait and smoke, and finally Wessi stops talking.

The dogs try to bark as the two vehicles roll towards us. The Nazi has two guys with him. We're outnumbered. But we have the dogs, even if they are muzzled. The Nazi glances quickly at the gun in my hand and the corner of his mouth twitches. But he's not worried. He stands there, ugly in a similar way to the pit bulls he's buying. He gives an envelope to Wessi, who looks quickly inside.

They shake hands, the Nazi and Wessi, and Wessi gives the dogs to the Nazi's guys to put in the vehicles. They're scared of them, that's obvious, completely terrified. They snap the boots shut and get in. The Nazi nods again and they roar away. Deal done. I didn't have to do anything: Wessi simply wanted someone there, that's all.

'Do you want to know a secret?' he asks as soon as we're sitting in his crappy car.

He has to tell someone, Wessi must always be talking, he doesn't know how to keep his mouth shut. I don't react. I hope for the sake of West Germany that Wessi really is just a nickname. We drive off. I look out the window.

'Twelve thousand,' he says.

'Twelve thousand?' I say and Wessi nods.

'Actually fifteen, but he took three at once. Discount.'

'Twelve thousand euros for three ugly dogs?'

'They're gladiators.' he says. 'I turn them into machines, into killers. Each of them is worth five thousand. If they do enough fights, they can make double that.'

I don't react. We get out, fetch Bella from the boot. Wessi looks at me. He's annoyed that I'm not happier.

'There's a secret.'

'Wessi, cool it.'

'Do you want to know my secret?'

'I don't want to hear about your shitty energy drink.'

Wessi laughs and kneels beside his pockmarked dog.

'Bella,' he says as if enamoured, 'is the best trainer. Look: I've removed her teeth, because she was destroying everyone. Old Rambo, worn out. Now she's a teacher.'

And then Wessi lifts Bella's lips as proof. I've never seen anything like it in my life. Her healthy teeth, sawn off, ending just above her pink gums. White stumps with black centres. I can immediately feel the pain. I think of dentists, root canal treatments, pliers and drills. I've never seen something so perverse. Only a Wessi could do something so insane. I wonder how he did it, but then I feel sick.

'It's so she doesn't kill her students, get it? After three, four fights they're ready.'

I trudge two steps ahead of Wessi through the dark woods. I am shocked, Wessi can tell, he chases after me and tries to see my face. But it's dark and I turn away. The dogs haven't calmed down, you can still hear them barking, even though we're already deep into the woods. I stop and ask: 'How many dogs do you sell a year?'

'Ten, twenty.'

'That's a lot of money.' I say and Wessi nods proudly. 'And you're giving me a hundred and fifty?'

'For your first time. Also, you didn't do anything today.'

'I've listened to your crap.' I say and Wessi, in his jovial Wessi-way, says 'Ach' and thumps me on the shoulder.

I lie in bed and can't sleep. I stare at the blind. I attached it two years ago and haven't raised it once, it's always down, I don't want too much from out there finding its way in here. I lift it up and look into the darkness.

All around blank scenery. Flat fields, a few crippled oaks, crooked and rotten. Gravel in the camp, the paths shoddily asphalted. Four kilometres away there's a petrol station, a rest stop and hotel, and beyond that Kaufland. Here there is nothing but us. And of course the two eight-metre-wide strips of speed. I drink half a Tetra Pak of wine. Then comes sleep.

Life in the containers starts shortly before six. The alarm sounds, rain patters on the roof, machines switch on. The flickering of neon lights. Biscuits, coffee, clothes. Then I stand in the morning and smoke.

Suddenly Wessi comes up to me, cigarette in mouth. I give him a light. A colourful dressing gown, flip flops in the cold, Wessi looks like a cartoon character. If not accidental, it's a genius disguise. He pulls out a bundle of notes.

I say: 'Well great, this is what reunification has given us, we're doing business with Nazis once more.' And Wessi laughs and thumps me on the shoulder and hands me three notes. He wants everyone to see that we're friends, that we do business together.

'Wessi,' I say and pocket the money. 'I'm out. It's not right, you know, this is the kind of thing you go to hell for, I don't want anything to do with it.'

Wessi thumps me on the shoulder once more, although we're really not friends now, not even colleagues in his perverse sense of the word.

Every day forty thousand vehicles thunder past me. Of those, a quarter are lorries and make the floor tremble. All day alone on the road sweeper, flashing arrows, yellow stripes, roadworks signs. The screech of circular saws, the dust, the ringing in your ears, I hear it still in my sleep, like a siren. From autumn into winter, that's my work. Still thirteen days to Christmas. Still twenty-four years to retirement. I don't fall for every piece of bullshit.

M. JOSÉ GALEANO

M. José was born in Medellín, Colombia. She studied Literature at Universidad EAFIT and learned Portuguese during this time. In 2023, she published a book entitled *Cuerpo disperso. Textos publicados (1912-1935)* by Fernando Pessoa, translated alongside Jorge Uribe in the framework of the research project PORLIT-EAFIT. She is part of the translation collective *Lenguas de Agua*.

majo.galeano.agudelo@gmail.com

The Universe is Homeland

Translated from the Spanish, *El universo es la patria*
by Emilia Ayarza.

Every effort has been made to contact the literary executors regarding the inclusion of this poem in the anthology, with no response. In the light of promoting the work of our students in a non-profit volume, we publish it here.

I am this broad-bodied woman

hormonal, upfront

this woman with a solar system beneath her dermis

with her limbs, her bronchi, and her pen

                                        healthy;

this woman who cuts the veins of silence

to flow desperately.

I am this broad-bodied woman

this woman that does not believe in limits nor languages

that does not believe in four dozen national anthems

nor in settled flag colours.

this woman that breathes with general air

that enacts the human song

the worldly brother

The cosmic man

the colourless child

and one and only flag

white as the dwarves' salt

white as the blacks' cornea

white as the whites' bones

white as the milk the Lapponians drink

collectively white

decidedly white.

I am this broad-bodied woman

who lives among the human race

who sometimes cries tears of Argelia

or shakes to the beat of Chile's gasps.

This woman who stays awake in Congo

who is hungry in China

who hesitates to close Pearl Harbor's scar

who loses sense and notion

before the c-section that cuts up

Berlin's golden womb.

This woman who belongs to Moscow's moon

                                        domain

who has Switzerland's calm languor

the colour of Colombia's melancholy

or New York's grey scandal.

This woman who owns the sea, the earth,

the sky, the wind, and the stars

this woman who kisses the mouth of the mute

who cries through the sockets of the blind

who screams through the cancer of men

and spreads a symphony among the deaf.

This woman full of love

who flows through the fingers of her hand

through the threads of her brain

through the hanks of her hair

through the milk of her breasts

through the mile of her skeleton.

This woman full of love for hate and vigil.

For death and abortion.

For Imbecile's mother.

For Mediocre's brother.

For Abnormal's father.

For Murderer's son.

For Impotent's girlfriend.

I am this broad-bodied woman

hormonal, upfront.

This woman with big laugh and border teeth

declaring definitively

from the loving territory of her heart

The Universe as Homeland!

ANNIE GRANGER

Annie is a translator, knitter and dawdler based in Norwich but raised in Southern Ontario. She graduated with a BA in Philosophy and French from Cardiff University with honours for her dissertation retranslating Monique Wittig. She translates French and German into English.

grangera42@gmail.com

In the Boat

The first half of a short science fiction story by Geneviève Blouin, originally published in French in *Solaris* 229 (winter 2024), and soon to be adapted as the short film "La Barque" by Productions Montagnes Hallucinées (2025).

In the grey light of an overcast sky, a boat rocks gently on the waves. Stood precariously balanced on the bow, a man studies the horizon made white by a thick mist, searching for a sign of salutation or danger. Three women, curled up in the stern, study the man. The fog seems to cling to the buckles of his breeches. He has lost his tricorn hat and his golden buttoned vest has been abandoned on his seat. Their companion in misfortune was a member of the crew; they knew of him during their passage, at least by sight. They could have fared worse.

With a resigned sigh, one of the women, the eldest, wrings out her long silver-streaked plait over the side. Another woman, a young girl, tries to affix her torn veil back on to her hair. The third, of middle age and with the appearance of a respectable matron despite her damp attire, watches debris as it passes by, aided by the current: a basket, a barrel, a lace-adorned blouse…

The barrel knocks against the hull of the boat and the man at the bow turns quickly.

'What was that?' he asks.

The matron shrugs her shoulders.

'Just a cask, M'sieur Ligny.'

'Not a…' he begins to say uneasily.

He looks around him. The undulations of the water create a movement in the fog. He is unable to discern anything, and this visibly distresses him.

He continues, 'Not another survivor?'

This is not what he had intended to say, none of the women are fooled, but they do not reveal this. They have known for a long time to feign ignorance when men are afraid or emotional.

'No,' says the eldest, 'there'll be no one else.'

The man clenches his teeth and fists.

'And how do you know that?'

'Because we hear nothin'.'

The young girl, abandoning her efforts to cover her hair to spare her modesty, goes on to say:

'Marie is right. There was screaming at the start of the night, but it's been dead quiet for hours now.'

She pales slightly once she realises the word she has used. Used all too well.

'What in God's name has happened?' laments Ligny sitting down on the thwart of the bow.

The women look at one another. It's not exactly complicated...

'The ship sank,' says the matron.

'I think he's aware, Agnès,' says old lady Marie.

Ligny takes his head in his hands.

'A brig of that size should not sink like that, not without raising any alarms!'

'I noticed a significant amount of alarm,' observes the young girl.

Ligny raises his eyes towards her, his brows darkening. The tone of the remark was halfway between factual and facetious, as if the young girl were mocking him. The face of the sailor soon softened, unable to believe that such a frail maiden would dare laugh at the situation.

'I was speaking, my dear Tara, of the alarm that ought to have been raised before the sinking of the ship.'

The young girl swallowed at having been addressed in this way by the sailor, with a familiarity and possessiveness as insidious as the hand which, only two days prior, he had slid beneath her skirt during an encounter on the narrow staircase to the hold. Ligny remained unaware of her distress, no doubt having plunged himself into his recollections of previous disasters. Being a sailor by trade, it is not the first time he had seen a ship in trouble. Usually, from what the women have heard, the lookout spots a reef, or the men in the hold notice an ingress of water, then the entire crew scrambles to save the ship.

'This time,' continues Ligny quite suddenly, 'there was a sudden flood which submerged the ports despite the hold being dry. Then we sank as one, as though a demonic hand was pulling us to the bottom!'

Demonic. The word has been said. The women guess what will follow. They look about themselves. Water and fog as far as the eye can see. Nowhere to go. No help to hope for.

'There must have been a witch amongst the passengers!' declares Ligny. 'A witch who has brought this misfortune...'

Young Tara's eyes widen, Agnès' lips purse, and the old lady Marie lowers her head in dismay — for who is in danger when witchcraft is suspected, if not old women? — only to raise it again soon after, resolved to defend herself, to alter the course of events that had been set into motion and of whose final outcome she was fully aware.

'Or perhaps,' she exclaims quickly, 'the captain should've listened to the warnings and avoided the northern Anitcôte Channel? Everyone knows it to be brimmin' with sea monsters.'

In a rustle of wet fabric, Tara lifts her knees on the bench and hides her face in her skirts as she whimpers:

'I've seen them. While we were fishing you out the water, Marie.'

Agnès nods gravely. She, too, had seen frightful shapes in the shadows and the mists.

'They've had a shipwreck feast, no doubt about that. And what a waste to boot! Crossing the ocean to die in the Gulf.'

Ligny furrows his eyebrows, a man clinging to his ideas and recalling his Catholic catechesis. According to the parish priests is it not women, and especially witches, who are responsible for all the ills of humanity?

'If there are monsters, it would be... be because the witch summoned them!'

There it is, always the same explanation. After all...

'Everyone knows that monsters fear the divine light of the celestial spheres,' Ligny adds heatedly, 'they never show themselves without persuasion, which is why we see so few. That's why people believe them to be made-up.'

The women exchange worried glances. This reasoning never bodes well. Old lady Marie purses her lips. A breeze begins to blow and the mist shudders. Splashing noises. The craft is jostled by a series of ripples in the water. Marie, Agnès, and Tara huddle close to one another. Ligny tries to look everywhere at once without losing his balance, but he suddenly wobbles and has to drop to his knees in the boat to avoid toppling overboard.

Just then, a few cubits from the craft, a tentacle pierces the mist behind him. The three women watch as it rises into the sky, as if to greet the dawn, then falls back down — *flak* — with a strange, flat sound.

'What was that?' exclaims Ligny, turning around.

All he sees are concentric rings on the surface, already fading into the swells of the rippling water. Tara and Agnès look at Marie out of the corner of their eyes, and she is the one who replies to the sailor:

'Nothin', M'sieur Ligny. It's just the breeze pickin' up, that is all. The waves must be hittin' some debris.'

'Something came out of the water!'

'Nah, we would've seen it,' says the old lady.

Ligny glares at Tara, then Agnès, and asks:

'And you? Did either of you see anything?'

Both shake their heads without hesitation. This does not seem to provide any comfort to the sailor. He runs his hands over his face and through his hair, causing his coiffure to come undone. He suddenly looks older, as if worn down by fear. Or struck by madness?

'Because if it is the monster,' Ligny mumbles to himself, fingering the cuff of his shirt, 'it means it's still hungry, that it's not yet appeased, that the witch... the witch..."

Marie closes her eyes. Tara stifles a groan in her hand. Agnès clenches her fists. They knew it would come to this.

'The witch must not have perished,' Ligny continued, 'She must...'

He returns his attention to the three women.

'She must be on board with us...'

Suddenly, he picks up an oar from the bottom of the boat and uses it to point at them, accusatory:

'It's one of you!'

Marie recoils as though having been struck. Tara cries out in fear and cowers against the matron. Agnès wraps a protective arm around her and places her other hand upon the old lady's shoulder.

'Stop this! You're terrorising the young girl, and you'll cause the old lady's heart to give out.'

Ligny draws himself to his full height and strides menacingly towards the stern, oar brandished before him, ready to strike. The women have nowhere to run to escape his attack... But his movement unbalances the boat. It pitches, and Ligny almost loses his footing again. He lowers his improvised weapon a little and tries to apply a veneer of gentleness to his combative posture.

'Ladies, do tell me which of you summoned the demon,' he coaxes, 'and we shall throw her in the water to chase the monster away. The other two need not suffer. With the monster gone, the mist will surely lift, and I shall lead you ashore and protect you. And young Tara, if anyone should speak ill of her for having spent the night in my boat, I shall marry her, fret not, I shall...'

'And what if the fog don't lift?' interrupts Marie. 'If the monster don't leave?'

'Why should it not leave once its hunger is satisfied?'

"Cause if I were a monster summoned by a witch, I wouldn't want a meal of witch,' says Marie.

Ligny opens his mouth, like a fish surprised at having been caught.

'Yer story don't make sense at all,' the old lady continues, 'Y'want to chuck me in the water, I've understood that, 'cause I'm not as pretty as little Tara, or as marriageable as Agnès. Y'see me as dead weight, so by callin' me a witch, y'think you'll be rid of me. If it calms the monster at the same time, it's killin' two birds with one stone. I see right through yer game, Mesieur Ligny. Y'ain't the first to try.'

MEGAN HARVEY

Megan is a Sheffield-born translator with a background in publishing and foreign rights. She reads, translates and re-creates French and Spanish writing that explores the connections and tensions between humans and the natural world. She is currently based in Norwich, UK.

meg.h2294@gmail.com

Ironwood

The opening extract from a work of prose poetry
Bois de fer by Mireille Gagné (2022).

1.
If one day you were to tell me that I was going to metamorphosise into a tree, I would throw myself into researching each species and their characteristics extensively, looking for the one with the hardest heart.

2.
It all started a few weeks ago. Appearing out of nowhere, these marks, so many marks. Yellows, mauves, reds, scarlet, orange. Despite all my subsequent efforts to get back to my skin, in every sense: spraying it with bleach, soaking it in OxiClean, scrubbing, the bruises will not disappear. The complete opposite in fact, they are intensifying with my therapist.

3.
How to even describe the feeling: extreme fatigue increased tenfold by the presence of invasive parasites. A pest, there is a gypsy moth laying her eggs in one of my crevasses, she is pulling out the coarse hairs around her abdomen to protect her offspring. Touching those fluffy masses will lead to breaking out in hives. To be rid of them, the nests must be destroyed one at a time, the bark must be washed with soap and water, the young must be drowned before they make more of their own.

4.
Nevertheless, I keep going, I am persisting, I am relentless, I am chopping away the wood until there is nothing left, I am slipping on my most sparkling exterior, I am staying close to the ground when you visit. It is easy to camouflage my marks, I am diverting your attention elsewhere, to the sky, to the squirrels, to the disease of my neighbouring tree, to the flower that is about to be trod on. I am dreading that you will lie me down on the ground, that you will dissect me under the light of a magnifying glass. I have never really understood *small talk*.

5.
You are speaking of me as a lime tree. I am growing much too fast for my commercial potential. My branches are pushing so high, so far, that one day I risk being split in two by one of those furious northerly winds passing through.

6.
With the hope of reviving myself, I am swallowing all sorts of well-advised organic mixtures, vitamins, both colourful and colourless tablets. I am cutting out gluten, soya, rice, corn. You are all so worried about watering me. Just give me some space, grant me some earth, a field, forest, an island for me to take root in.

7.
This apperception of asymmetry is not pleasant. I am never fully satisfied with my foliage, with my rectitude. Always worrying about being degraded. A witch's broom is sticking up from somewhere behind my neck. My bark is pulling between my shoulder blades and collarbone. Despite making every effort to let go, I am always catching a surface, your eye, a pool of water, a memory, a window, where my image is reflected, incomplete.

8.
I lost my essence. I doubt that any of you noticed, as if my intimate aroma had slipped out through a tiny lesion whose existence I had been ignoring. Since then, I have been afraid of becoming lost among all the woody scents of the neighbourhood, of not finding my own trace.

9.
You dream about putting me in a pot and taking me indoors for the winter. No doubt you have convinced yourselves that I would be able to purify your inside as much as your outside. You are forgetting something crucial: trees also need relief.

10.
The anxiety is dense. This suburb is packed up with echoes, silences, static. My body is recoiling, adopting these inextricable positions. My vertebrae are tightening, compressing, shifting. The weather is getting raw. My leaves are retracting. The chiro is never finding the right knot. He is insisting on swings and bird feeds when all he should do is prune me. I am nearly touching the electrical wires.

11.
I am going to see different specialists. I am desperately tackling all the dark spots on the wood, the nicks, the grubbing, all the scree and abatis. I am getting the aphids removed with acupuncture. Nothing is working. The pain is coming from elsewhere. Seeing does not reach the essential.

12.
I have heard it said that the acacia, which grows in South Africa, possesses a unique characteristic. Raided by antelopes, it is releasing ethylene as a warning to its neighbours. Upon receiving the message carried by the prevailing wind, the nearby trees are immediately enriching their leaves with tannins that make them toxic to predators.

13.
If only I could pick up the signals of distress around me, of sensing which parts of me risk being eaten alive. I fear that the enemy is already hiding within.

14.
My yoga teacher is repeating tirelessly that I must find my inner calm. I must inhale fully, allow the air to get in through the openings and fill the body, layer by layer, first the bark, then the phloem and the xylem, right down to the core, hold it for a few seconds, then exhale slowly. Finally feeling the letting go. The difficult part comes after.

15. Eliminating a few insects;

16. Bandaging the bark;

17. Twisting a branch;

18. Splitting the trunk open;

19. Extending the roots;

20. Clearing myself of rodents;

21. Swallowing the stop sign;

22. Ripping out the gutter;

23. Breaking off a piece of asphalt;

24. Knocking down a bit of foundation;

25. Making a list of tasks which would give me back a sense of freedom.

26.
It seems that ivy is emerging from anticipation. Once germinated, it is never stopping in its course, it is creeping up the length of the trunks with its aerial tendrils, it is enveloping and asphyxiating the lower branches in its filtering out of the sun. Its weight is making the tree more vulnerable to being uprooted by the wind, the strong rains, the snow or the ice. No matter how much horticulturists insist that it would be wrong to call it the executioner of trees because it does not actually kill them, do not be fooled by the greenery and its ornamental yet persistent leaves: the berries are fatal.

27.
This dread of not dropping my leaves at the same time as the others and leaving the bulk of me uncovered.

28.
I am being careful to keep the hundreds of bird skeletons out of your sight. Each autumn, as I start to deplume, an indescribable panic takes over me at the thought of someone exposing them to broad daylight. They would make such strange jewellery.

29.
The softest places are always on the inside. The nooks where the wood is beginning to rot from within. To repair them, I start by searching for a hole. From the tips of my fingers, I do not always find it on the first go. My hands are moving all over my body until my nail catches on the bark. Sometimes the hole is big enough to get my thumb in: it is usually a squeeze; I have to really force it in to make the gap wider. Most of the time it bleeds, it screams. I am plugging it with twigs, with silk, with dead or wounded animals.

30.
The opening always ends up closing again, leaving only a fibrous scar on the surface, another growth ring on the trunk to remind you all of my break point, my alterability.

31.
Since when was it exactly that you started your nighttime visits? Set up in a watchtower hidden behind my hair, you are being recklessly loud, scanning the forest day and night waiting for a beast that does not come. You are impatient, anxious, swearing, breaking my epicormic shoots, firing from midday to make the children and crows scarper.

32.
It is just as well that, in these rare moments, my leaves are aligning and I am glimpsing through a crevice of light. A ray of sunlight is bursting through and, in a fraction of a second, it pierces the unattainable.

33.
At other times, the rain is so forceful that water is getting inside. There is nowhere dry to take shelter, the faucets are flowing freely. Long rivulets are getting in through the cracks, the fissures, the grazes. The bark will not hold out much longer. Water is pissing from my branches. It's surging out of the tiny orifices in my roots. It is making my bones dilate, saturated with rain. In these instances, if a stethoscope were put to my trunk, the sap's ascent would be heard. I must not be tapped or have a spile attached to me. I risk being emptied out.

34.
Mushrooms are now pushing out all over. Artist's bracket, silver leaf, chicken of the woods on my trunk, under my armpits, in my mouth. They are smothering all outside sounds. I am dreaming of a child, a deer, a woodpecker to swiftly clear them off me, putting a stop to this slow digestion that is making me rot and disappear bit by bit.

35.
On some mornings, the clearfelling leaves me feeling depopulated. All around me the logs are corded, so many lives slaughtered. The wind, the sun, the rain is perpetually pelting me. I always believed that to maintain equilibrium, some shadow proved essential.

36.
As soon as I scream, it starts again. I am discovering another cavity that I did not know I had. I have a bad feeling that you are set on digging some tunnels inside me to fill your pockets with sawdust and shavings. I am imagining you, getting home in the evening, busily compacting them into logs and, when comfortably sitting by the fireplace, watching them burn with satisfaction.

37.
'It's time to start scarification surgery,' my therapist is convincing me. He is explaining that this forestry treatment involves disturbing the humus layer and the rival low vegetation to loosen the mineral soil so it can be mixed in with the organic matter. The procedure is simple but painful. Once it is over, still quite shaken, I am looking into the gashes. I am apprehensive about what they will give me access to.

38.
Once the insecticide has been sprayed, it is impossible to predict the number of insects who are about to be ousted from the nest.

39.
Surviving extinction, surviving extinction, surviving extinction, surviving extinction, surviving extinction, surviving extinction, surviving extinction, surviving extinction, surviving extinction, surviving extinction, surviving pissing dogs, surviving extinction, surviving extinction, surviving extinction, surviving extinction, surviving extinction, surviving extinction, surviving extinction, surviving extinction, surviving acid rain, surviving extinction, surviving extinction, surviving extinction, surviving erosion, surviving extinction, surviving extinction, surviving extinction, surviving extinction, surviving winter, surviving extinction, surviving extinction, surviving extinction, surviving extinction, surviving extinction, surviving extinction, surviving extinction, surviving in sterile environments, surviving extinction, surviving extinction, surviving extinction, surviving extinction, surviving daily annihilation, surviving extinction, surviving extinction, surviving extinction.

JON RUSSELL HERRING

Jon is a writer and translator working from Spanish and Portuguese. He was Poetry Translation Centre's Queer Digital Resident in 2022, and a winner of the 2023 Stephen Spender Prize. His translations of Argentinian poetry and Brazilian fiction have appeared online, and his experimental autofiction piece *Quartet* was published in May 2024.

jon.r.herring@gmail.com

The Haven

A translation of the short story 'El Remanso' by Argentinian writer Inés Kreplak, taken from her debut collection *Mirar al sol* (2021).

She'd always vowed never to set foot in a casino, yet here she was, heading for Palermo Hippodrome in the middle of a storm, in pursuit of the phone she'd left in a taxi minutes before. Franco was still fully dressed but she'd had to throw on jeans, gumboots, and her dressing gown: she looked like she'd just come out of an improv class. They'd been forced to break off what they were doing when, as Franco was pulling off her jeans, she noticed her phone wasn't in the pocket. They rushed down to see if the taxi was still there, maybe stuck at the lights on the corner. But the second they got outside, they realized their plan made no sense.

Mariana opened *Find My Device* on her laptop: her phone was stationary at the junction of Libertador and Dorrego a few blocks away. Thinking the taxi might be at the rank outside the Hippodrome, they dashed over in Franco's car. If they could only find the driver — he wasn't picking up but wasn't rejecting calls either — maybe it'd be a quick fix and they could get back down to business.

It took two minutes to get to the Hippodrome. Pulling up alongside the line of taxis, they peered at them through sheets of rain, but none was hers. She checked the app again: the phone was somewhere over on the other side of the avenue. While the lights were red, Franco swung around and stopped next to a lone taxi parked with its lights off. Mariana got out to take a better look. No one inside, but through the back window she spotted her phone in one of the footwells, blinking. Each time the screen lit up, you could see the pop-up she'd just activated on the app.

As Mariana hurried back to Franco, it started to hail. When horseracing started going out of fashion, the Hippodrome had decided to install hundreds of slot machines. Franco looked at Mariana: 'We can't just sit and wait. Those guys can play all night. Do you remember his face? Would you recognize him?'

Mariana didn't answer, suddenly remembering the moment her eyes had met the taxi driver's in the rear-view mirror. Without looking up, she asked if he'd go inside.

'Can you remember his face or not?' Franco insisted.

Mariana said she thought so, noncommittally. It was clear she should be the one to go in. She grabbed the umbrella and got out, circling back to the taxi to check the dashboard. She memorized the driver's ID photo and name: Rodolfo Benítez. Once the lights changed at the crossing, she ran across Libertador, weaving between puddles.

Sheltering in the entrance, she re-buttoned her jeans, adjusted her dressing gown, smoothed her hair, and approached the first staff member she could find. Mariana was surprised nobody looked her up and down or seemed to be judging her outfit. Security, receptionists, cashier: nobody cared. She tried to explain what had happened, how she'd ended up in a casino wearing her dressing gown.

'So I think Mr Benítez is inside. Is there any chance you could make an announcement to let him know the girl he just had in his taxi is waiting out here?'

Mariana paused and smiled, trying to look sweet and friendly, suddenly realizing her breath probably smelled of beer. The assistant mirrored the sweet smile and replied:

'I'm afraid we're not permitted to disclose our customers' identities.'

Mariana did a nervous little laugh, not understanding.

The assistant told her she could go inside without buying any tokens, so on impulse Mariana went through. She would scope out the whole place looking for Benítez.

Inside it was dimly lit and she could only see people's faces at close range. Of course, she hardly knew Benítez at all, had no sense of his mannerisms, nor the way he walked. She also had no idea if he'd be playing the slot machines, at the bar having a drink with friends, or even on a date.

She wandered through the crowd, checking the face of any man who looked sixty-ish, with graying hair, a bushy mustache, and glasses. The place was a lot bigger than she'd expected. She had a sudden notion that if she played, she'd win, and then she'd have no need to find Benítez. She could just buy a brand-new phone, the latest model. But at the same time, she'd made that vow...

Her mother Paula was the black sheep of the Murphy O'Reilly family. She'd only been briefly married to Mariana's father, an actor working on the Fringe, and she herself taught sign language. While the rest of the family appreciated what a noble occupation this was, none of them could understand why she didn't just do it as a hobby, and more to the point, why she had to work as hard as her husband, if not harder, for them to get by. A beauty like her could easily have been a model or at least married someone more in keeping with her class, as Mariana's grandmother Bárbara always used to say. Uncle Alberto, on the other hand, had always been the grandparents' favorite. He had become an accountant, and it was he who managed The Haven, the property the family owned outside the city. But after their grandfather passed away, Uncle Alberto began to show his true colors. He had no qualms about losing twenty-five acres of land at the casino in a single night, even though it wasn't his alone to gamble. Grandma Bárbara protected her first-born, turned a blind eye to his waywardness. She lent him money, concealed his debts, and called in favors from friends to cover up all the scrapes he got into.

Mariana spotted a man in a white shirt with his back to her. She paused next to the machine and said:

'Rodolfo?'

The man turned and stared. She jumped: it wasn't her driver. She apologized and fled through the banks of machines. She continued looking for Benítez as she ran, but all she could see were women, much older women at that, and suddenly she was right at the exit.

Two security guards blocked her way. One grabbed her arm.

'Where are you going so fast, miss?'

Mariana apologized and explained she was looking for her uncle, she'd lost sight of him a moment ago. The guards told her to stop running around, she could get hurt.

'Look, you can't play chase in here.'

They pointed up at four CCTV cameras monitoring them in real time. Mariana apologized again, and as she moved away, she checked their belts to see if they were armed.

In the ranch at The Haven, there was an armory, where rifles, shotguns, and pistols were displayed in locked, glass-fronted cases. They also kept cleaning paraphernalia and ammunition of assorted gauges in the cupboards there. Her grandfather's hunting trophies — a variety of stuffed deer, boar and puma heads — were mounted on the walls.

The first year after grandfather's death, the whole family was at the country house to ring in the New Year. In line with custom, they started drinking early and in great quantity. Uncle Alberto got into a huge fight with Aníbal, his younger brother. According to Mariana's mother, Aníbal insisted they'd named the first lamb that was born on the estate Laurencia, while Alberto forcefully countered this saying no, she'd been called Argentina, 'it was "Argentina" after our great nation, goddamn it!' and continued repeating this at the top of his lungs. The argument escalated further, with Alberto telling Aníbal he'd always been a momma's boy, had never gone out to tend the livestock, was clueless about shearing sheep, milking ewes, and slaughtering animals. Aníbal replied with chilling composure that he knew for a fact that this particular sheep had been christened Laurencia as he'd heard it directly from their father on one of their secret cinema trips.

Alberto completely lost it. He stopped caring about the damn sheep's name and shifted his focus to the hitherto unknown bond between his younger brother and their father. Bárbara tried to intervene, but the yelling reached such a pitch that she eventually announced she was off to bed. The daughters-in-law and Mariana's mom observed the argument in silence until Alberto grabbed Aníbal's arm and marched him to the armory, where Mariana and her cousins happened to be playing a board game. What happened next became a recurring nightmare for Mariana. Her uncles bursting in, shouting, the moment Alberto got Aníbal in a headlock and put a revolver to his forehead.

'Say "Laurencia" one more time and then see what happens!'

As the words reverberated again in her head, Mariana steadied herself against a column. She was ashen.

'Sweetheart, are you okay?' asked a heavily made-up woman in a miniskirt. 'Hey, let's go and sit down on these little chairs over here.'

Mariana didn't resist. The woman's perfume was strong, a fusion of melon and violets that tingled in her nostrils. She had long acrylic nails, immaculately painted in a red that matched her lipstick. After sitting Mariana down, she told her she'd go get her a glass of water. Mariana shook her head. She wanted to say something but felt too weak. The woman took Mariana's hands in hers.

'Sweetheart, I need to get back to the old guy over there, real quick.'

Mariana looked across to where a graying man with a paunch was playing on a slot machine, eyes unblinking. She turned back to her guardian angel.

'What have they given you? Why are you dressed like that? Do you want me to call someone for you?'

Mariana tried to speak, to explain, but the woman didn't let up.

'You shouldn't be here. These security guards are tough guys. Please don't stay much longer or you might get into trouble. Take this, and get in the first taxi you can find out front. Don't forget your umbrella.'

Mariana held still as the woman moved off toward the old guy at the slot machine. She watched her kissing him on the lips, putting her hand down his pants. The guy stared at the machine, still not blinking. Mariana came to. She had to get a move on, she needed to find Benítez and get out of there. Outside, Franco was waiting for her, and a storm was raging.

She managed to stand. At first, she felt dizzy, but then steadied herself. Over by the bathrooms, she saw three men in a corner surreptitiously stuffing money into different pockets. It took her back to the moment she'd stumbled on Uncle Alberto in the library at the country house, pocketing something he'd taken from one of the drawers. In her head, she heard his words again as he'd pressed coins into her hand: *here you go, get some candy, but it's our little secret, right?* That was Mariana's final visit to The Haven. They'd been forced to sell it not long after.

Mariana pulled the money the girl had given her from her pocket. She sat down at the first free slot machine she found, convinced she'd win and be able to buy back the house. She fed it peso after peso until she had none left.

She got up from the stool and blundered through the aisles, looking down at the carpet in case anyone had dropped any money. She contemplated selling her watch, wondered how much she'd get for her ring... Then seeing a sign for the exit, she realized it was all madness and she had to get out — but she couldn't run with those cameras on her. She eventually found her way to the emergency exit. There was a thunderclap outside. She tightened the cord on her dressing gown, flung the door open and stepped out. She put her umbrella up and picked up speed in the rain, running blindly. She had to find Franco and get home as quickly as possible. Pausing and taking a deep breath to compose herself, she set off running once again.

PARIS JONCHIER-LITWACK

Paris translates from French (fittingly) into English. Phase one of her academic venture at UEA (BA in English Literature with Creative Writing) was spent grappling with her identity as British-born eldest daughter of French(-Vietnamese) and American(-Puerto Rican-Polish-Lithuanian-Jewish) parents. Phase two (operation MALT), as it turns out, isn't so different.

paris.jl@outlook.com

That Man's Mother

A translation of 'La mère de cet homme-là,' a short story by Lucile Bordes, from her collection *Aurélie et autres femmes sans nom*, published by Éditions Thierry Marchaisse (2022).

The census lady hands me two sheets of paper. We look at each other. We know each other, everyone knows everyone here, and our address, our story — well, let's just say there's been enough media coverage to know where we stand. Still, I somehow pluck up the courage to ask her for an extra sheet for my son.

You not giving me another one, for my son?

Her fingers clamp down on the forms. She hugs 'em close to her chest, like a child.

Caught her off guard, that did. She doesn't how to answer — can't quite bring herself to say no. Doesn't quite know *how* to say no. We're in the kitchen, where I showed her in not five minutes ago, a couple feet apart. I watch her as she tries out sentences in her head and mulls over how best to avoid giving it to me, that sodding sheet of paper. 'Course, all those sentences could fit into one, one apparently too hard to say out loud.

Your son's in prison, he'll be counted there.

She can't say it. She knows full well he's in prison, we both do.

He was like plenty of other kids, my kid. You know, the ones who don't really like school, but who don't draw attention to themselves either. Didn't speak much. Didn't like it. Gets that from his dad.

His big sister was a different story. She was a chatterbox. She couldn't sit still. She had friends. They were more important than anything to that girl, those friends of hers. She'd rather piss herself than risk leaving 'em for more than two seconds to go home to use the toilet. She's like the bloody Duracell Bunny, their dad would say — we had no idea where she got it from, all that energy. We'd catch her on her own in the garden, running, jumping, nattering away as if there was someone else there with her. It was like having a caged animal for a kid. All her brother ever did was watch quietly from a distance. Not quite happy, not quite sad. Grew up lonely. It was my mother-in-law who made him that way. I didn't really get a say, you see — she decided I wasn't cut out for it when she saw how bad of a job I'd done on the first one, who was so bloody exhausting. She'd say it to her son, too: she's no idea what she's doing. As I said, I didn't get a say.

Truth is I *was* exhausted. I was having seizures and the epilepsy meant I had to quit work at the factory. But the children never went without. My husband was a bricklayer, he worked hard, plus we had his mum's pension.

At the trial, they racked their brains trying to figure out why my son did what he did. So did I. I still can't make any sense of it. I think he must've got it like I got epilepsy. Experts said he'd been a *child in need*. None of us knew what that meant. It means he was *deprived*, the lawyer explained. Deprived? We're not deprived, objected my husband. Not deprived as in poor, clarified the lawyer, deprived as in emotionally deprived. My husband wasn't having any of it. His voice echoed through the courtroom as he told 'em he'd always been there for his son, that he could always count on him. Could've heard a pin drop. The air felt more breathable after that. I saw my son's back straighten slightly. He couldn't look any of 'em in the eye, all those people who'd come to see him, now that he was what he was and no longer the kid they once knew. But he straightened up a bit, so I did too, stand up straight, I told myself.

That kind of criticism would've killed my mother-in-law, had she still been around to hear it. The woman had no time for nonsense. Feelings? Yeah, she didn't really do those. I couldn't cuddle the kids without her pulling me up on it. Had to brush their hair in secret. Coddling 'em like that won't teach 'em anything, she'd spit out. We felt ashamed whenever she'd catch us. It worked, in the end. As soon as they were old enough, one after the other, they started doing things her way.

So, while we might not have been big on hugs, or words, my husband was right about one thing: we'd always been there for 'em. Even now he was into his thirties, even on those nights when he'd piss his pay up the wall, my son knew he'd always have his place at the table and a bed to sleep in. He'd lived on his own for a bit, when he started working as a labourer, but he came back home once he got a job here. We had the room. There were only three of us left: his dad, him, and me. His nan had died, and his sister had gone to live with some guy. We got on, the three of us, never had any problems. And we had more than enough words for what we had to say to each other.

They appreciated him at the factory. He was thorough, my kid, hardworking too. Never called in sick. No one saw it coming — his boss said he never would've expected it from him, not in a million years. I didn't see 'em coming either, the coppers, that day I swung the door wide open for 'em, just as I did earlier for the census lady, cause even though I'm all skinny now, I'm still in the habit of doings things the way I did back when I was fat, before I lost all that weight, before all the heartache. I've shrunk. Wasted away in just a couple years.

Anyway, fat me swung the door wide open, and when the officers asked after him, I worried there'd been a scrap at the pub, since he *had* seemed a bit on edge when he got in (as the papers reported the next day). I told 'em he was downstairs, in the garage. The officer in charge signalled to his guys and half of 'em shot down the front steps to corner him round back of the house, where they found him trying to mount the fence, to get to the forest through the neighbour's, I suspect, cause it's really close — so close that we sometimes get animals coming into our gardens in winter. They put handcuffs on him. He was handcuffed at the trial too, to begin with. Didn't change my kid's face though, those handcuffs — he still had his good old face, always watching, waiting. What did he do, I asked the officer.

I don't think he ever answered me. We have to ask him a few questions, he said, we'll keep you informed.

I ended up finding out through other people. Through the eyes of other people — the eyes of our neighbours, followed quickly by the eyes of the nosey, once word got out — told me all I needed to know. We were animals in our neighbours' eyes, cause that kid had come from us, and that man had come from that kid, that man that wasn't a man at all. The nosey lot probably expected us to drool, or wail, to be marked, you know, in one way or another. They were disappointed when they saw we were normal, resented us for it.

The neighbours' eyes went away once they announced the verdict. They wouldn't look at us after that, it was as if it hurt 'em, as if we were contagious and they risked catching it, this sickness of ours, just by looking at us. Not one of 'em said hello anymore. They'd cross over to the other side of the road as soon as they saw me or my husband coming, hurried home the moment we showed up anywhere. They didn't dare pounce without the rest of the pack. It was only when they were together that they'd pipe up, cut short their conversation just so they could swear and spit at us as we walked past. These were people who'd been to ours for drinks, mind you! People we'd helped out. These weren't people who didn't know us. But that's exactly what they were telling themselves, that they hadn't known us, that we'd pulled the wool over their eyes, that we'd tricked 'em, that we'd hidden it from 'em.

They really were like dogs. Growling and afraid. They couldn't face us, went sniffing round behind our backs instead cause they didn't have the nerve to do it in front of us. We'd have shooed 'em off if they had, with a stick, a shout, but they came at night to write their crap on our wall and bang on our door.

My husband lost it one night — wanted to take the gun out, to scare 'em off. I'll fire into the air, he said, watch how quickly they scurry away then. Wait, I said, just wait. It's a good job he listened, cause you could hear 'em all outside, baying like hounds. That's when it clicked for him: he wasn't the hunter this time, but the hunted. God only knows what would've happened if he'd gone out there.

They were the real animals. They wanted us to pay for our son. He hadn't done anything to 'em. These people, they took 'emselves for vigilantes, said that, thanks to him, no one would ever see the village the same way again. These were the same people who'd gone blabbing to the journalists first chance they got, getting their photos taken where it happened and all. Always the same pose too, looking serious, left hand pointing at a bit of wall, or pavement. They'd do anything for their fifteen minutes on the telly — make up stories, come up with theories, said my son had tarnished the image of the people round here. Dogs.

I realised, seeing 'em chase those mics, that they envied him. The kid existed in a way they never would, and he'd done it overnight. Maybe that's why he did it, to feel alive. I blame myself for that. I didn't see it, that he wasn't *living*. I didn't want to see, or I forgot to. That he wasn't interested in having any friends, that he didn't have a girlfriend, I acted as if it was his choice. I didn't want to push him, he's like his dad — doesn't like talking about himself, only ever spoke about work. But I knew deep down, and his sister would tell him too, when she came over, on Sundays.

He did it to exist, I told my husband.

Someone must've got in his head, he replied.

I didn't say anything, but I can't see who, he never saw anyone. Even at the pub, he'd get annoyed if people talked to him too much. Yeah, no. This was life's doing — it'd taken its toll on him in a way we never could've expected. That's all there was to it.

I don't need those dogs to tell me I should be ashamed.

It was over that day, for my husband and for me. Our past, our future, it was as if none of it had ever existed. All of it had been cremated, reduced to the ashes of what we were now: the parents of the man who did that.

I can't get used to it, this cremation.

I may be that man's mother, but he's still my son.

That's what I say to the census lady, before she has a chance to leave without giving me his form.

She doesn't answer. Lets her eyes trail over the wallpaper by the front door. Horsemen on a foliage background. Doe and stag on a foliage background. Hounds on a foliage background. Deer. Horsemen. Deer. Dogs.

How many? Never counted.

After a while, she gives in, hands me the sheet of paper, and we write my son's name on it together.

ELIZABETH LUTZ

Elizabeth translates from Swedish to English with an interest in poetry and children's literature. She has a BA in English and Scandinavian Studies from Gustavus Adolphus College in Minnesota and an MA in Literary Translation from the University of East Anglia. She is also an enthusiastic knitter.

elutz777@gmail.com

Source text © Ingrid Sjöstrand – Licensed through ALIS.

Maybe It Matters to You

Selected poems from *Angår det dej kanske* **by Ingrid Sjöstrand**

Maybe it matters to you
what I do?
And what I think?
Maybe it matters to me
what you do?
And what you think?
Maybe we matter to each other?
You and I and all of us
who happen to be living here
right now
with the world hanging
on what we do
Maybe we matter to each other?
Maybe yes
Maybe

The cat walks around the house
planting flowers in the snow
— Yes he does!
Haven't you noticed
that every step
leaves a flower in the snow?

I'm the only one who's me
I'm the only one who thinks
and feels exactly like me
I'm the only one who sees
myself in a puddle
in just this puddle
in just this street
just now

What if it's not even there
if I only think that it is
What if everything is like the cinema
and I only b e l i e v e that it's there?

But I'm in the film, right?

And I know that mama's there, right?
If she's only in my head
wouldn't she be how I want
— never scold or nag
but always think the same as me?

You can't think about someone
who isn't really there
Maybe...
But how can she think about me
if she isn't r e a l like me?

Except you're never sure
I'm the only one who's me

Tomorrow I turn eight
That'll be fun you know
Maybe I'll get the next Meccano
the one with more wheels
Maybe I'll get the Beatles' latest
though it's expensive you know
Why am I so sad?
I'll get cake probably.
Tomorrow I turn eight
and will never be seven again

The worst thing about mama is
that she always has advice
for everything
If I say
that everything is lousy
that I don't want to go to school
that I hate Kenny
that my new sweater scratches
she says
that it will be better in a while
that yesterday I liked Kenny
and take another sweater
You don't even get to feel lousy
in peace

Sometimes in the garden
when I was six
I stood against the wall
and unzipped my fly
and stuck out my finger
and pretended to pee
like a boy
What if someone thought
that I was a boy!
Just think if anyone saw me!
I would have died

My big brother has a moped
and his own tape recorder
those are the things he tinkers with
that give him a contented look
He has oily jeans
and is always black around the nails
He sunbathes under a blanket
and wears long trousers the whole summer
He can turn a Marie biscuit
whole in his mouth
He plays chess with me
One time I won
because he messed up
he said
but I was no birdbrain after all
he said
that time I won
He drags me down the basement stairs
and binds me in one motion
— if I struggle there'll be a flood
he says
He goes to the library for me
when I have a cold
he tosses the books onto the bed
— You're welcome, little brat!
he says
My brother is a softie

Sometimes I dream about skeletons
that just force themselves on me
closer and closer
I shout
and wake up
— It was only a dream
says mama.

How does it help
that this darkness was inside of me
and not outside

CAITLIN MCKIE

Caitlin is a Scottish literary translator who works primarily from Norwegian. She is finishing her MA in Literary Translation, having completed the undergraduate degree MA (Hons) French and Scandinavian Studies. She has a keen interest in translating literary fiction that is 'emotionally charged and introspective,' and is still figuring out how to make that description more specific.

caitlinmckie1216@gmail.com

Be My Baby

A short story by Kristin Vego, from the collection *Se en siste gang på alt vakkert* (2021), translated from Norwegian.

At the bar where they meet, flowers hang in glass vials from the ceiling. He's been out for drinks with his colleagues, and she's in the city for a seminar. They start talking.
   'Are you often in Oslo?' he asks.
   'No, it's my first time.'
   On the speakers, rhythm and blues is playing. *Hit the Road Jack. Wild About My Baby. You Gonna Be Sorry. Fever.* They sit together, heads almost touching so they can hear each other. They go outside to smoke.
   'It's much lighter here than it is at home,' she says.
   He smiles, as if it were a strange thing to say.
   'It is light.'
   They go back inside and buy another drink, sit down again, heads almost touching. And then they leave. Out on the street, a blanket of fresh dew has settled over the people and cars.
   'Shall we walk for a bit,' he says.

He works in an office in the city. At the seminar, she listened to a presentation on ethical hacking, and did a workshop on social engineering and data security. Their first kiss begins so: They come out of a newsagent and stand quiet next to each other. She turns towards him, slowly, just as he resumes conversation. She moves her feet, hips, and shoulders, so slowly that you wouldn't know it was on purpose, until she is standing right in front of him, her body right up to his. He's taller than her. There's a small pause in the conversation, she can see that he's weighing it up. Then they kiss for a long time; he was the one who kissed her first, and she was the one who got him to do it.

He sits on the edge of the bed with his jacket and shoes on. Fresh air streams in from an open window.
   'Thanks for last night,' he says.
   He brushes strands of hair off her face as she wakes.
   'I've left a spare key for you on the kitchen counter,' he says. 'You can just put it in the mailbox when you let yourself out, but sleep some more.'
   For a second, she sees his eyes flicker, as though he regrets what he said (after all, he doesn't know her, he doesn't know what she might do). He gets up to leave for work. She smiles at him from down under the covers, a smile that says: You can trust me, you know me now, in a way that only a handful do.

Sofie stands up, discovers that she's naked and finds her underwear on the floor. She has no desire to put on her shirt, or her jeans that are too tight; they smell of sweat and alcohol. She can feel it now in her body too, that she drank too much last night, and she smoked, which she doesn't usually do. In the wardrobe, she finds a pair of joggers and a band t-shirt, with a name she doesn't recognise. It is late morning. She goes into the kitchen and studies the Nespresso machine a while before she figures out how to work it. On the fridge, there are photos of his kids he told her about. Sofie can't remember what they're called. They are both smiley and light-haired. She takes her cup of coffee into the living room where there's a sofa and bookshelves and an indoor palm tree. A castle made of Lego sits on the dresser. On the wall, there's a painting of a woman walking in a field.

As she stands in front of his mailbox by the stairway, she reads his name several times. The key to the flat remains in her pocket, or his pocket; she's still wearing his joggers and t-shirt. She walks outside, into the morning traffic where a blue tram has stopped, letting people off onto the platform. Now at the hotel, she packs up her things and checks out. The plane leaves in three hours. With her suitcase rolling behind her, she walks back through the city, through Slottsparken and past Litteraturhuset, letting herself back into his flat, locking the door behind her.

Her books will stay on the left-hand side of the desk, just beside his. Her clothes claim an empty shelf in the wardrobe, and she finds a hanger for her silk shirt. She takes it all in: her new home. Her toothbrush finds its place beside his own and the two smaller ones, in the toothbrush holder. She slots her suitcase under the bed before she makes it.

Sofie opens the door to the children's room: a bunk bed, a desk with a desktop computer, and on the wall, a Liverpool F.C. scarf. By the window sits a small collection of figurines with big heads. On the floor, there's a plate of crumbs which has maybe been there several days, so she takes it to the kitchen and puts it in the dishwasher.

Hopping down the stairs two steps at a time, she stops by the mailbox. With two bits of tape from the desk drawer, she attaches a small piece of paper to the upper right corner. First there is his name, written in ballpoint pen, and underneath there is hers.

She exits onto the street. The flat is located right by Bislett stadium, the air is warm, and there are people in the cafés and at the tram platform. The city is full of light and of things that shine: the tram tracks on the concrete, the porcelain cups at Kaffebrenneriet. A window glints in the sunlight as it opens wide. She walks through the city and reaches the river. Follows it to its waterfall and then further up to the grass, where dogs run freely. On the way back, she spots someone on the other side of the street. A woman with two kids. They have blond hair, walking with school bags on their backs. Their mother has a hand on each shoulder. They're his kids, Sofie thinks. She winks at them, but they don't see her.

She reaches Vinmonopolet just before it closes. While she stands there in the queue, with an expensive bottle of Italian red wine, she hears someone say her name.

'Sofie, hi.'

Sofie turns around. It's Jenny, she went to school with her years ago.

'Hey!'

They hug.

'What're you doing here?' Jenny asks.

For a moment, Sofie is confused.

'I live here,' she says.

'Oh, you don't say!'

Jenny works in the city as an architect. She speaks quickly, talking about everything that's happened since last time. Sofie listens as she looks her over. She's wearing a dark suit with matching trousers, and knee-high boots. Around her neck, the thin gold necklace that Sofie remembers from school.

'Do you live here alone?' Jenny asks.

'With my husband and his kids,' Sofie says. 'We live just up the street. You should come by sometime and have a drink.'

She holds the bottle up between them.

Sofie pours some wine into a glass and lets the calm sink in. She walks a turn around the flat and turns on all the lamps. She likes switching the lights on when, in the summer, it starts to darken. She can see a fragment of the city through the windows; a flock of pigeons who land to rest on the church roof. She sits down on the sofa, putting her legs up, twisting her ring slowly round her finger, something she does often without thinking about it. The washing-up sits untouched in the kitchen. It's been a busy day.

Sofie closes her eyes and notices immediately how easily she could sleep. She takes a sip of the wine and leans back into the sofa, warmth flowing into her fingertips. He'll be home soon.

She stands in the hallway as he comes in.

'Hi darling,' he says. 'Sorry I'm back so late.'

'That's alright.'

He sets his bag down onto the counter and hangs his jacket up behind the door. He wraps his arms around her waist to pull her into him. Sofie leans in against his neck and smells his skin. He kisses her on the ear, forehead and then lips.

'I got you some wine,' she says. 'The nice one from Montepulciano.'

'Lovely.'

He smiles, takes off his shoes, and follows her into the living room. Rests a hand on the back of her head.

'How's it gone with the kids?' he asks.

'They're asleep,' she says.

Sofie opens the door slightly to the children's room. There they lie, one in each bunk, their delicate hair splayed out over the pillows. They sleep so sweetly.

ANA SOPHIA PLATT

Ana grew up in Stavanger, Norway. Her love for studying world literature started at her international high school. Today, she studies Literary Translation at the University of East Anglia, working from her native Norwegian to English. For her dissertation, she is translating her grandfather's memoir, which depicts his experience with the Norwegian Resistance Movement during WW2.

anasophia.platt@gmail.com

The Ghosts of Frost Island: Behind Death Mountain

A translation of Chapter 37 of the book *Spøkelsene på Frostøy: Bak Dødsfjellet* by Hilde Hagerup.

We threw ourselves into the hole and crawled behind Finn's cage.

He looked up. 'What's happening?'

'They're coming!' Wilma hissed.

Finn ran to the front of the cage and started hitting the iron bars. The other children did the same.

'Go away! Away with you! Whatever you are! We're not afraid of you.'

'QUIET!'

It was my grandmother who came first.

I'd never seen her like that. Her eyes were glowing. In her hands she had a long, grey chain. The curly hair no longer sat tight against her head but stood straight up. As if she were not a ghost but an animal.

As she screamed, the children fell silent. Only Finn remained standing with his hands around the iron bar.

'You don't give up, do you?' my grandmother said.

'Never,' said Finn. 'I'm going home to my sister!'

'We'll see about that,' my grandmother said.

'You know it was a ghost who let them out?' Finn said. 'Is there anyone you can't trust?'

My grandmother hit the iron bar with the chain. 'I said QUIEETT!'

I don't know if Finn was about to say something else, because they were interrupted by a man in a black cloak who appeared right behind the Duchess, hovering.

It was Count Stefan.

My dad.

He was standing just a few metres in front of me. Was it true that he was evil? Was it true that he scared human children to stay alive?

It was hard to believe, but I knew it had to be that way. Not the one with the ugliest screams. Not the scariest looking, but still one of the worst.

Grandmother turned and nodded. None of them said anything until Johannes came. He didn't fly, he came on foot. And he was carrying something in his arms.

If it hadn't been for the arm dangling on the ground, I might have thought it was a bundle of clothes, but it wasn't. It was the boy from The Other Island.

'Name?' Grandmother commanded.

'Albert,' said Johannes. 'Eight years old.'

The Count went over and opened Albert's mouth with his finger. Stefan looked up as he ran his fingers over Albert's gums, thinking.

'Okay,' he said, eventually. 'Cage four.'

He tried to take Albert out of Johannes' arms, but Johannes wouldn't let go.

'Wait.'

'Why?'

'We made an agreement to change the routines.'

'Yes,' Stefan said. 'And you have, haven't you? You haven't gone bragging about your catch to all of Blekbo this time?'

Johannes didn't blush with anger. He didn't turn white either. He turned grey. If my grandmother hadn't been there, I'm sure he would've hit Stefan.

'Stefan takes him. Cage four. That's how we've always done it,' Grandmother said.

Johannes spat on the ground.

Albert whimpered.

'We've got more important things to talk about,' Grandmother continued. 'Someone needs to train Jens, otherwise we'll never get The Other Island working again. Max said there were even more pictures there last night.'

'It's no use teaching Jens,' my father said. 'He's never going to help us.'

'For once I agree with the Count,' said Johannes.

'What we need is better security. I was thinking ab–'

'It's no use thinking,' Johannes hissed. 'You've got to do something too. You can't just stand around planning all the time.'

Stefan pretended not to hear him. 'We've got to use Arnold Blek's own system. Then there's no room for small children.'

He turned and looked at Johannes. Johannes looked at him. They stool like this for a moment in complete silence. Then Johannes dropped Albert on the ground.

Even though he was cruel, I couldn't bear to watch my father get beaten. But he didn't seem to care. His mouth turned red with blood, but he only gritted his teeth.

'For goodness' sake, stop!' Grandmother roared. 'Don't you realise that someone's been talking?' she continued. 'How did they find out about the Ice Rose on The Other Island? There are bonds between the living and the dead. That's what it's all about now! We have to find that nasty little... Wilma.'

The Count stopped grinding his teeth. Johannes nodded and lowered his fists. I breathed again.

Wilma!

I thought about what Finn had said. He wished he'd known her when she was alive. I did too.

But would she have been my friend then? I wasn't so sure.

'And your wife,' Grandmother continued and spat at the ground by Stefan's feet. 'I said it before at your wedding. In my speech! You're not just marrying the person you're in love with, you're marrying a whole family. And the family marries you. And look what we got! Look at the crap you brought in, Stefan. I'll never forgive you for that.'

I felt a knot in my stomach. Mum! They were talking about Mum!

Stefan just shook his head.

'Has anyone seen Wilma yet?' he asked.

'No,' said Grandmother. 'She's been gone since that day–'

'Yes, the Ball.' Johannes interrupted. 'But we've seen traces of her. She's been in Hans' pantry and stolen some pickles.'

When Johannes said 'pickles' both he and Grandmother laughed.

'Olga thinks we can use Jens as bait. We're working on it. She's somewhere in the house, we know that much.'

I looked at Wilma. Had she been living in hiding since we arrived at Blekbo? How had she managed to do that?

I took her hand and squeezed it. She didn't squeeze back.

'And what about your wife?' Grandmother turned to the Count. 'Where's Lucia?'

Stefan shook his head. 'I don't know where Lucia is. We've been in the house several times. Cornelius has searched the forest, but she's gone. It's a mystery. We saw her on her way here just after Jens arrived, but since then we haven't...'

Mum! I was both relieved and scared. She had been trying to find me. And the ghosts hadn't managed to find her yet!

But where was she?

'I told you I can send Angelica if you need help,' said Johannes.

'We don't need help,' Dad said.

'Are you sure about that?' Johannes snapped.

'It doesn't matter who does what,' Grandmother said. 'The important thing is to cut the ties. To do that I need a cool head, Stefan. A ghost who can think.'

She smiled. Just for a moment. At least I thought she did.

'I've been thinking,' said my father.

'Surprise, surprise,' said Grandmother.

'Arnold Blek's own system...' he began.

But he was interrupted by Johannes, who started laughing.

Hysterically.

His eyes glowed.

Yellow.

They looked like they were crackling.

Like he had fireworks inside his eyelids.

Fireworks that were about to explode.

'Ha! Ha! Ha! HA! Says you! Who dragged a living human child into Blekbo?! Let him experience the Ball of Death?! The Other Island even! What were you thinking of doing with the ties between the living and the dead, you said? A ghost who THINKS? Because thoughts can move mountains, can't they? Stefan? Or was it not like that?'

Grandmother looked at Johannes. 'Do you want to know what we've been up to? If Jens can't be used as live bait, we'll send him out into Frost Island Forest. He gets one job. Find the Ice Rose and destroy it. And then Stefan will kill him. Jens becomes a ghost. Just like you and me, Johannes. That's Stefan's plan. You're a smart ghost, Johannes, but you're only fourteen. There are some things you have to leave to the adult ghosts.'

Johannes trembled.

I couldn't move. They weren't going to lock me in the dungeon like they did with the other children. They didn't want to feed off my Fright — the sticky green substance that ghosts ate to stay, well, alive. I was going to die! That was Grandmother's plan.

I was so nauseous it was hard to breathe. Then Wilma started moaning next to me — it wasn't a low or soft moan, but a loud and plaintive one. So loud that we had no chance of staying undercover.

'What was that?' said Count Stefan.

Johannes ran around the cage.

Wilma was crouching, still moaning.

I knew she was sick. Just not how sick.

Johannes pulled her to her feet.

'It's the human child and... Wilma!' he cried.

Grandmother grabbed my arm so hard I screamed. 'Don't you remember what I said?' she hissed. 'You have to trust me, and I need to be able to trust you. If you make a choice, you must stand by it. But you don't, do you, Jens? You're a feather in the wind. Suddenly you're here, suddenly you're there. Is it so hard to decide?'

'No,' I said. 'Not any more.'

I looked Albert in the eye. It was Grandmother's fault he was here. He and all the other children.

'You're evil,' I said.

I spat on the floor in front of her.

She laughed, her mouth wide open and her rotten teeth on display.

The music in the background had got louder. Piano. Faster and faster.

Grandmother wasn't a ghost. She was a monster. Now she had to yell to be heard.

'Johannes!' she screamed. 'Start with Albert and throw Wilma in the cellar. Stefan, you take Jens. Empty his pockets and take him to the Room. He can sit there while he gets tender!'

I felt a pair of adult arms lift me up. It was my father throwing me over his shoulder. And then I realised something I should've realised a long time ago: I'd never had a father.

CHRIS SALPINGIDIS

Chris is a translator of all trades and master of none. His primary trade bridges Greek, German, and Swedish to English and vice versa. He is currently undertaking an MA in Literary Translation to learn how to build better bridges.

c_salpingidis@yahoo.gr

PROLOGOS, EPEISODIA A & B, EXODOS

Translated from Greek, four poems by a kind heart, beautiful mind, and dearest friend: Yuri.

PROLOGOS:

Maybe bad days
co-ordinate
to stretch and bend,
prod and press,
tighten and pull
a heart
until it's taken
the shape
it was meant to.

EPEISODION A — PHOBOS:
A Swan Landed in my Garden

A curse
to live as the vessel
of every first thought —
Shades of morality, decency,
pulsing colourblind.

In class,
unaware of who's looking,
he'd let his finger-
tips drift
south
under the desk
to stroke his jeans.

Scenarios of carnage,
cornered.

Heads —
An amalgam of guilt and fear
breaks out,
sheds his body,
and gathers its books and notepad in a hurry.

He'll find some excuse. He'll run home, push the bolt shut, and crawl into the foetal position.

Tails —
An amalgam of guilt and fear breaks out
until he manages to pull his belt off.
Tails.

EPEISODION B — ELEOS:
Mischief

As soon as your back's against the door,
behind it, you'll find me in bed
shamelessly stealing
the warmth you left
on your side.

The blue of dawn,
stealing through the curtains, hesitant,
colours in a Thursday lying on the back
of every Thursday
past.

Your side grows colder,
the blue grows grey.
I, in deep mischief,
seek some thrill

in the heartbeats and sweat
the spit and bruises,
stay.

EXODOS — CATHARSIS:

I'll be reborn —
unwaveringly incomplete,
in colour replete
or not,
never new —

till all my lives and deaths
are spent,

as long as you love me
exactly the same
every life.

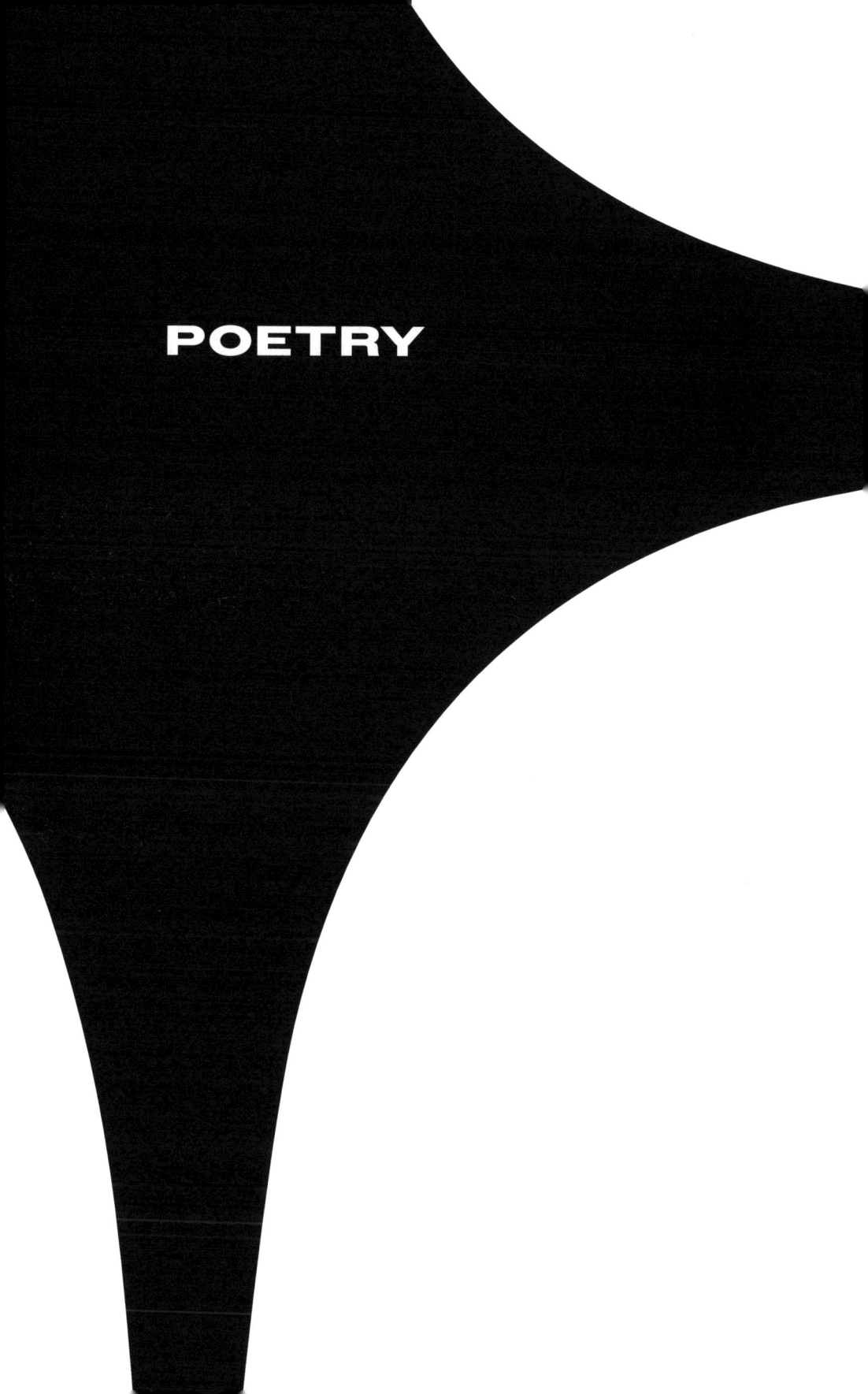

BADRIYA ABDULLAH

Badriya Abdullah explores the diasporic nature of her heritage, having grown up in England to Tanzanian parents. Winner of the Rebecca McMannus Prize and receiver of the Birch Family Scholarship, she invites her readers on her journey to unravel her experiences as a Black, Muslim woman in the UK.

zaynobe@gmail.com
@Badriyaishere on Instagram

Oranges with Bibi

Don't hold the knife like that!
the first love lesson
from my grandmother.
[Imagine it was in Swahili, I don't
want to cheat, you see.]
The knife was now more dangerous
waving around in her hand
punctuating every syllable
as she punctured the air.
Tizama she said as she
held the orange in her hand,
kama hii, na peel.
She slipped the knife under
the skin, twisted the fruit
and it followed her lead
without resistance.
You could have been a surgeon Bibi
a laugh as fresh as the juice
echoed across the waves
and a perfect peel landed in the sand
usi sema nonsense!

Messy, kama Swahili yako,
she chuckled. The second
love lesson, don't take
her teasing to heart.
My turn made short
fat pieces of peel
fall to the ground.
Practice makes perfect, and
watching her hands
was always easier than
watching her lips. My fingers
always twitch but my mouth
could stay forever unused.
Listening can take you far, hear
the agreement of *eh-heeeeh*
or disapproval of *ah-ahhhh*
but for all I've listened,

I could not tell my bibi,
that I love her in Kiswahili.

How is your Swahili?
[imagine Swahili]
Alhamdulillah, nzuri a little.
It's been ten years and
we still can't hold
a conversation without me
slipping into English.
Lete chungwa.
Something I understand, so I
glide the blade under
the skin, twist until
a perfect peel falls
on the ground,
slice the orange in half
juice catching in
a small bowl- no, *bakuli.*
Wewe unafanya vizuri.
Asante Bibi.

Dear Babu

For the first and last time, we met in Zanzibari sun
hot sweetcorn in hand and motorcycles run-
ing like sparrows. We passed flowers; cause of death: gun.
"To Allah we belong, and to Him we return."

You spoke to your daughter more than me,
the six-year-old with inadequate Kiswahili
but I asked what if our paths would no longer meet
"To Allah we belong, and to Him we return."

Since you have entered death, Mama has bowed her head
in prayer constantly. Eyes vacant like yours which led
me to ask why the extra devoutness during pain. She said,
"To Allah we belong, and to Him we return."

He was a strong runner, Auntie said off
the cuff. From hand to hand, the relay baton of
news spread and each pair of lips joined the chorus of
"To Allah we belong, and to Him we return."

Now it's a regular phrase, whenever I need to praise
you and the things you've done. Ten years on, I raise
my head to the Zanzibari sun, and listen to the waves,
"To Allah we belong, and to Him we return."

to reverse the effects of colonialism

we divide the tongue between us
mash the muscle into taste
buds and pho ne tic al ly work
our way through the fields
our foremothers left behind.
we did not know
the dirt was sullied with salt
until two winters passed
when the buds bore no fruit
clung to their mother
never dropped into gaping
mouths. no ancestral gut guided us
we were starved
of sound into silence.
maybe in this wasteland
we could hold each other close
grow into a new tree of sound
of speaking. Mother Heritage
would you bring us home
if our roots could siphon life
from yours?

On reading 'On Seeing the Elgin Marbles'

I tell Keats to get a grip
that mortality weighs upon everyone
that his history is still here for people to see
and still stolen.

No statues will be put up in my people's honour
the museums of my homeland are bare
robbed of scraps to fill the pockets of the living
history doesn't feed starving mouths
his luxury tears water empty lands.

I tell him his past still shadows
the compass that will take me home
with my ancestors tied
to my back like children
soothed to the sound of
usilie. Hamna baraka
kwene tears yako
lete mie hopes yako
dreams yako.

DANA COLLINS

Dana was a recipient of the Foyle Young Poet Award in 2019 and a runner-up for the Wells Festival of Literature Young Poets Competition in 2020. Her work can be found in the Young Poets Network, Little Stone Journal, Viridian Door, and Graphic Violence. She can be found online @danaishpastry.

danado.collins@gmail.com

fester

        child purulent and blistering
              left to grow
                        my rape on a petri dish

          pick the mould
      from dinner   still can't finish the plate

            tears like butter pats   in jacket potato
        mum says come home

             but child is sticker residue
        everything
        clings
                      pores are
                someone else's

     child at home
     mouth sutured into solid lip

different
      never clean
  sheets
                      changes
            everything
                    dirtied

      face disintegrates to chalk
             skin like   gratings

        child must
  sweep up the flakes   eat them

                 filled with the rot

child is always child
child is always at home

                child

                                  body

          is

                                  is

                    touched

Funny ha-ha!!!!!!!!!!!!!!

Crack open a tinny except
there's no fizz!! Knock it over
I scuttle out, all-fours and cackling.
Everybody's day is ruined!!

Learned to knit for my godmother
still dropping stitches. Looks like shit,
all unravelly. She'd love her scarf
if she weren't too dead to wear it!!

My ancestor once stepped on a snail
now it's like my voodoo doll!!!!
Ugly mosaic of snapped-up
spine and snail home!!

Paid a lady to watch me rearrange
my guts, now my mouth knows
only raven-speech. 200 pints in debt
still a big fat loser!!

Wait for someone to laugh, except suicide
threats 'aren't funny?!' Have you heard
the one about nooses???? Please
don't leave me hanging.

some of me

creature scoops out mug
                        guts
                                         finds
                                            fingerful of petrol

                flecks of
                skin on skirting
                board amalgamate
                into   mountain

                                  berefted gaps of body
                                  writhing
                                      intestinally
                                        into bed

empty
        water glass crusts   next to pothos
                                              fit for bin bag
                                              burial

creature with plughole hair
                        stares
                        at
                        walls

                                                          this is all.

Return 2 Munkie

                            lacking a cock
                                  dripping in gumption

I hike up
    skirt like   ripping off
                          skin
flatten hands
against cool basin   hoist
                          self
onto
  sink
        all lady   like

                    anatomy is a barrier
                          like tomatoes are a fruit

      knees bent
      ankles   cuffed   soft
                              polka dots

find my balance
                                              piss

SARAH HULME

Sarah Hulme is a poet based in Norwich. She was long listed for the 2023 National Poetry Competition and has had previous work appear in *Foxglove Journal, Now Then Magazine* and *Ink Sweat and Tears.*

sarlou.hulme@gmail.com

After

they planted me my veins
grew split my sky hung in
sighs the violet of kissing
skin & occasionally every
thing was aflame like the
curl of her tiny fingers—

Coast

A string of houses pegged sky to horizon, where black was falling deep blue. My feet sank, my breath fogged, the wind rushed then rested. The moon was faint, a sliver of another wakeful night spent watching. A V of geese strained eastwards, their flaked chatter hung like snow and then a single goose, about a thumb from the end, reaching, now an index finger, reaching, now two hands, reaching but falling, falling behind. Not one waited. Not one looked. The gap grew as they slowly trailed out of view. I turned left, leaving the beach and its bands of yellow to the sleeping sea. A line of trees, framed by another line of trees, pining for the sun souped rays of summer, skirted the dunes; the first natural defence from a ground turning inwards. A shadow lay about a foot from where I stood. It was small, no bigger than a new-born baby, silently frozen in an angled violence I was glad I had not been there to witness. I was beckoned forwards, towards the shadow, away from the sea of boom of rumble of salt. The shadow was perfectly

> *I lived on the sea*
> *borne to a world*
> *shift from warm to warmer to*
> *day is sick, slip of oil slick*

still.

Bruise

Your soft landing of too
       much blue. Drowning in hot

    cotton. Fossil of dream-
  imprinted purple I

          am a room of meat you
    are holding me o

     pain.

MEIER SMITH

Meier Smith is a queer songwriter and poet with a distinctive confessional, rhythmic, and lyrical voice. She is a Young Norfolk Laureate, won the inaugural Writing Award at the Young Norwich Creative Awards in 2023, and was longlisted for the National Poetry Competition in 2023.

meiersmithpoetry@gmail.com
linktr.ee/meiersmith

paving way

if i feel a young pulse from my wrist
i might end up five again, tasting bed-covered
air straight from its cocoon & becoming light
for the first time. *if you press beam against skin, you shine red.*
time clenches stomach each second
until another tooth falls out, until coins cross-pollinate
under my pillow, until there are none
more to lose.   i am always empty & willing
                  for something to be more than me.
when i was seven i needed me now i've taught myself how
to cradle the purple of her.
sound out sorrow's shape, the word
'knife' from her curled tongue.   *draw triangle of a father.*
i'll watch her at three, shoving his wooden edges
into a circle, bringing all corners of the room together. she doesn't know
to enter the sheet, turn it inside out & cover the cold
of six. she assembles a home from jenga, hugs each piece with her hands
& always takes last. always the slats under her mattress.
always sinking or gathering
herself together. hiding thumbs in her yellow ruched skirt, tucking hair
into curls, slowing rain into dimpled
concrete. i watch them now–   rushing down my drains   filling out
years in a second & swaddling the oxygen of my newborn crib.
it's never enough to blow out my candles, grow out another pair
of shoes, wear my big sister's manners, see the final stream of light pick
through the window, blinds
turn inside out, lungs
cry themselves in, eyes
fall back   into a torch.

playhouse

i've got a whole box dedicated to letters my dad sent me that i won't dare read again but won't dare bin he thinks i'm still wearing purple groovy chick tshirts & choreographing dances to my sister's ipod playlists he doesn't know that i'm wearing bleached lungs he doesn't know that my fireplace cries bricks out & he's never had to buy me an umbrella not even a flimsy one he's never had to knock on my front door or see my surface tidy kitchen he's never lit two numbers on my birthday cake or smelt the smoke from the hallway every day just feels like another step towards being someone he wouldn't have to wash spare sheets for another day of unlearning his voice so i wouldn't know it on the phone so i wouldn't know he hasn't been calling

in grave

                i am so good   with a chisel   i can just keep tapping away at the rock

      friction burn my skin like a bumper car that bumps all over the walls

                antenna clinging to your spine

so if i take out bricks we'll go with them   how many bricks does it take

        to sound the cliffhanger buzzer   become that game where you're the circuit

            energy grounding & i'm always on the wire setting you off   i drag

    down your metal lines   trace each curve   thread

      my needle like a seamstress lowering   her pinch

          realigning each   puncture   to follow through with intention

              measuring an inch between the tip

of my thumb & knuckle   grazing scabs where a thimble should

  be   i'm collecting each dress i make from your bones so i know which sizes

     of you i'm yet to wear   or which one i wore first that made me feel

the smallest inch of myself   i leave room in me for a zip or button loops

   so i can be undone   watch each day back in live photos

    holding the screen just a one-inch step   from my face   pointing

       my past self back at me like a gun

gag on ur good

a death wades any city
& trains us how to cross a bridge
& pay our entry grief
& say each word of forget
& keep googling more ways to
& send more flowers in text
& burn our mother sky until it tears nightless
& thunder ourselves to sleep
& dream we can see the bombs diving
& tuck our legs into our chest
& stay fetal in our white sheet womb
& watch a father carry small limbs in a bag
& be happy we saved ourselves first
& feel the ash sweep into our throats
& taste the smoke of another falling
& stave off the smouldering toothache until morning
& wake to thank god we're not really there
& know we have no reason to be scared in the dark
& keep our cheeks planted in heavy snow
& say if my mother had sadder teeth maybe i'd bite down
& gag each train off its tracks
& run out of places to be holy
& soon be back on January's hardwood floors
& syringing thick drowning into my mouth
& shooting gratitude up my arms
& charging my battery devotion
& remembering again how to swallow it all back down

PAUL MARTELL

Paul Martell was born in Norwich and studied Business Finance & Economics at the University of East Anglia, later completing an MBA (Banking & Finance) at Exeter University. He writes about everyday moments to preserve them like collectible postcards.

paulmartell@btinternet.com

Rose Valley

Just off Unthank Road, our street
began where the Tavern now stands.
There were nine of us at number fourteen
a terraced house, two bedrooms, a box room
a single mattress near the wall.

The kitchen below was fitted
with a copper clothes boiler
fuelled by coal and a wall oven for baking.
A sting of hot soda water and damp linen.

These were days of hand-me-down clothes
scrap meals of stewed bones and dripping on bread
with homemade cakes to fill our stomachs.
I shall never forget my final kiss on his face
as he lay in his coffin and the anguish I felt.

Bernard, our baby brother scalded by a kettle of water
kicked from a hob off the burning fire.
The visit of the coroner's officer
the inquest and funeral haunt me still.
The houses are all gone now.

Showbusiness

Not all fryers keep their vows
but I take my work seriously
frying chips is not as easy as it looks
crisp outside, soft on the inside
the colour of straw is the aim

The hot dripping and neon lights
kept us nest warm inside but the streetlamps
unhid the dark drizzle of men lurching
in from the beer-cobbled night
clutching their fistfuls of greasy change

A crinkly bottom is best
a wink to the ladies here
world-weary in their big-buttoned coats
the missus wrapped red-raw hands
a fury of grease paper and condiments

Black hairs on the fryer's nose glistened
he laughed nervously, eyes darting from face to face
frying time is not the same as ordinary time
the woman in front turned, left without words
We all shuffled forward one

Eaton Park

Swinging without end
in that first awakening
beyond sky when
time was boneless.

Endless days knowing
nothing of what had been
or what might become
swinging high.

The world was young
with its bee-hive hair
cloudless empire-gone
never so glad days.
Times were once good.

Visitors in time and space
the past quietly etched
in the bark and branches of trees
stretching up like throne bearers.

Hardly more than a girl herself
pushing me towards
the drone of being.

TABITHA BENNETT

Tabitha is a human person who writes poetry and very rarely biographies. The following poems have no conscious connecting theme, and she cannot comment on her work as a whole without being woefully vague or inevitably contradictory. She will say that 'spittle' is a great word, with an unfortunate meaning.

tabitha@housestorm.co.uk

a gun is a rose is a rose

This poem takes inspiration from Gertrude Stein's title 'A rose is a rose is a rose' and Chabuca Granda's piece 'the poet's gun is a rose.'

grasp it tight and don't let go   raise your hands for the world and say this is my blood   see how i bleed   wont you bleed with me   and we offer our roses that aren't guns   relinquish them to un-thorned hands   and we shout our blood   smear it on the page   the world   my face   your face   our hands hold this rose that will never be a gun but a plea   poets have roses like america has guns   we will defend our right to bear arms   skin just laminate over veins   vines roots that twist and pulse with rose scented   rose blood   and the petals fall to our hands and they aren't petals anymore but blood   you tell me to fight   as if i haven't already died in combat   you hand me a gun that isn't a rose and tell me to fight   except my thorned hands cannot hold it i am fighting   we are fighting   if you want to make change in this world you have to fight for it   you say   as if you don't see our blood on hands   faces   pamphlets   anthologies of blood that you don't see on shelves   in bookcases   in mouths   in hands   hands that hold roses   and blood   our guns are roses and we are at war   bring me a florist.

Day Today

      Hang

          Fold

                Fold

      Hang

                    Underwear

                Not mine

         Refold t-shirt

                        Planet friendly bag

                      Goes on my head

                  Naturally

                Segments glow

            Campfire through cloth

            I wonder how long I'd have to spend in here

          Before I went insane

    I draw a house

        And label it house

    I draw a path

        And label it path

    I draw a flower

        And label it flower

            The walls say   read me

            The rail says   hold me

          The service to   norwich

        Is calling at   norwich

              Blue silence of 3:50am

Your head is on my shoulder

My hand is in your hair

I think of heaven

And if I'll see you there

Your hand strokes my face

And I forget

Wandering

life would be so much better if i could whistle
i'd like to make my own birdsong
tabsong twining with beaked notes
brushing by twig tipped branches

what does a leaf think as it falls

does it

embrace the carrying winds
know it will hit the ground
care

will it

when a child giggles
as they step on it

strands lurch past my face
hair reaches into the wind
sun opens my eyes
and the world climbs in

recall feeling the urge to fly
so sure that i could
possibility tingling in every atom
i feel it now

but the wind dies
the suns grip loosens
now only gravity holds me here

MICHAEL ATHEY

Michael Athey is a writer from Northumberland studying the Creative Writing (Poetry) MA at UEA. He was awarded Highly Commended in the 2023 Terry Kelly Poetry Prize for his age category. When he is not writing he works at a second-hand bookshop back in the North East.

Contactable via: michaelathey@icloud.com

/andfi//ed

mate was fee/ing po/yethy/ene

                     p/astic disasda bags

                           c/ingy to his friends fi/m

                   fu//y

    semi-skimming   stone mi/k

                  drowning

                                     fizzed out pop

             head/ess & shou/ders

                                        /ego star

                                              warding away

mate was fee/ing po/ypropy/ene

                 spoon   knife &   forking he//

microwavab/e

                        b/ister pack

                                un/icked mü//er pot

mate was fee/ing po/ystyrene

dot

    dot   that no /onger fe/t /ike home

       dot   ted around the p/ace

                        from the wind escaping s/ashed tyres

             /ike mind spinning party p/ates

mate was fee/ing

         out into the dark

                  until he fe/t the razors

       & found

            a single use b/ade

    is mu/tipurpose

in the end *mate was fee/ing*

                                             biodegradab/e

Do you pay for your prescriptions?

door alarm wails
as if to say
a criminal

WARNING: he might try shoplift happiness

would if I could

    like

of course they're not actually that quaint
I have to explain to myself
again
how they work

    it's like
        it's like
my mind

    likes

to wander more when house sharing

the bathtub vortex is physically uninstalled
with doctor's gloves
and calmer waters
two tsps worth
their weight in gold
are transplanted in this
lilo
I lie on

    like
        like

an iron watery lung
each breath chemically measured
inflating
keeping me

       like

afloat

popping calmer waters
means I miss the superlatives

       like

the darkest of caves

the caves are still dark
but a knob of butter
melting tells me it could be darker

but also

       like

the belliest of laughs

a balance I swallow
                    daily
with tap water
write the letters of the day so I remember
with tsps of good humour

       funny
              not belly funny

how do you compress a feeling into a pill

       like

a colour to the mast? daily

and there you stand   m t w t f s s
doing your job
with a patient confidentiality stare   _ _ w t f _ _
asking
do you pay for your prescriptions?   "Daily"

Depression is a Villanelle

The truth is we just don't have the personnel.[1]

I've come to realise Depression is a villanelle.

Sometimes I pre-empt the lurch into the footwell[2]

The truth is refrain two is due anytime now as well.

A helical jumper of hand-me-down blood cells
sown to me with duvet claws.
Maybe my Mother was first to think depression is a villanelle.

My mind is harboured in the footers of unused shower gel
weighting down a two-month waiting list for a prescribed thaw.[3]

my friends try their best but they can't always tell.
"What you dropping out of the group chat plans for?"[4]

1 Stuck in a möbius hamster loop forever more
2 as refrain one returns for an encore
3 The truth is Talking Matters don't have enough personnel and
4 it will be a while before we discuss depression as a villanelle.

EDEN CHICKEN

Eden Chicken, born as Eden Gray, is a queer poet whose work generally focusses on hybridity — of form, of identity, and of existence in the natural world. Throughout their years of creative writing study at UEA, they have increasingly experimented to *play* with language and form, creating a distinct voice.

edenmcgray@icloud.com
@edenchicken [Instagram]

i wouldn't call myself a patriot

daddy   dad dee   dada day die   d da daa

                                                                                                    ta da!

papa fertile   or sh'ld be   promised green
& pleasant lands   not these days   did thou hear
our soil is decarbonating   degraded earth

papa farrow   bear forth thy last
name   pray for penised progeny t' bear forth
thy last name   infinitum 'til only daughters

papa fellow   a nod halfsmiled across th' street
a pint on th' table & a piss i' th' johns   not certain
i' thou voice w'ld sound i' my defence

papa fond   spread thy arms t' embrace
how much they can contain i' their expanse
how tight   how close they can hold one near.

BONE

flying fish ripple b'neath my spine
journey me moonwards
in   to the sweet exosphere
sticktongues me
ninthcloud icing sugar heavy
i am reverberating   w' everything
you say   what if
we meld to one
we try my back stacked against stomach
powdered/lubricated   you say
it's working
i've been drafting i' m' head
artiststudio / madmancave / traceysbed
∞ monkeys w' ∞ typewriters
—

a dry tongue strikes
every   vertebra
the mirror to
morrow—twisted
neck—reveals a burn
perfectly vertical
blisters tips t' th' touch
—

that night have t' sleep
facing   flatchest   down
like when you make me
yell slobb'ring   wetting the sheets
pillowswallowed hOwls
you keep on
pounding   panting
oblivious t' th' charred spine
warped i' front o' you
oblivious t' th' fish
carrying me   on
plunging th' salt's skin
from behind
hear you
come

IN MY BRAIN I AM THE CAUSE OF EVERY SINGLE PROBLEM I ENCOUNTER

my bi kwon't cycle
        & i excoriate myself
for not knowing how to ride
even aft i find — —   —   chainsfallenoff

                rain   ing   d   ats &
  dirty   c   ogs
rats
     haunt   memory   doggy
       strip muscle   bones dog tired
         flesh   world
                     marrow
maggots   sucked out of me
  skull   crawl
     sloppily
                       wheeling my useless self home
                          cheeks rusted by tears

let me   cinder my toast
      & pick skin to blood   high
      & drink too much   coffee
                           spirits

let me   unpick my seams
      gearshift &   pull out my inner tube
      & fall   to parts

                          mesh
                            flemory

crevise (vb.)

                rabbit on rabbit
                 over wet   grass
                verdant shot lick my
        wounds clean   pink tongue
        wet curl   kitten lapping milk
                  white splashes
               lick muscle   clean
                      bury
              your head   mkiss &
              into my crook   mcry
                bury   for you
               your hand in my
                     crotch
                   ety bitch
        cosy   outgrown cubs   settle
            & regress into my grooves
                  chalk teeth
              wetly   tongue scrape
                the sugar cubes
             clean lick   gritty lump
                   & shot &
                    mbury
                       ,

written by the window, smoke traversing thresholds
& skies mirroring my crepuscular temperament

i don't mind meltwater fresh skies,
   nose&cheeks flush numbpink, drag
     -ons breath, raindropped snowdrops,
       or the paraffin glow of spiced eves
        & homemade stars — i used to love
         how strangers' dinners wafted with
          my walk home, kitchens reeking of
           laughter from too many cooks. i don't
            mind huddling under heaters breathe
            in their smoke & lager, another glass
             of house red cheers, staggering streets
              to giggle at snow that might only be
               rain caught in lamplight. i don't like
                the dark still, its inky mouth gulping,
                 consuming the ordinary as early as 3
                  p m, the way i wilt pale ensnared by
                   circadian sadness, clockwork — let
                    me not always be the ogre at sunset
                     must the head peal w/o relent, the
                    calcium creak & cement in muscle:
                   delicate egoself shatters to eggshell
                  pieces that cut our thumb incarnadine.
                 i like the thickness of bedroom dark,
                bulk that i can bite back unlock jaw
               & shake the beast between my teeth
              like the dog i am lurching my fear
             towards unknown chirps & echoes
            burying my face into your nape, the
           dirt i dig up for my bone relishing
          moist warmth: flesh breath & earth.
         your hand secures mine, lurid orange
        streetlight beau_{ti}   _{bi}fy ing—
              ful ly   zom

T' Ode

1   spinewards creeping dark shivers / nothing breathsnatches like the expanse of fear like *freeze!* twig snapped / alone alone alone / a lone

2   spider (could) be coming to get   / nothing skincrawls like

3   o   ' ! lyttel tode mottled by metamorphosis and lakeness / bruisedpear hued
– *arwk arwk crkk crkk arwk awrk cr–*

4   paused stoic toes web/bed to earth / you are waiting   for me,
5   journey affected, disturbances on the track by a clomping fool / blithering blind

6   leave you be / a lone a lone a long all own alone on and on a

MIDORI TAKAHASHI

Midori Takahashi studied English education and worked as a teacher in Japan. She is a tanka (a fixed verse with 5-7-5-7-7 morae) poet, and her interest is writing English poems with tanka-like conciseness. Her poems are based on observations and reflections of her daily life in the UK.

moppet.takamido.evergreen3781@gmail.com

On Campus

Two sequences of tanka and one short poem based on my life in Britain

On Campus　キャンパスにて

1

the tranquil campus morning —
a small squirrel 栗鼠 crosses
right in front of me
straightening horizontally
its question-mark tail

ひとけなき朝のキャンパス疑問符のごとき尾を立て栗鼠の横切る

2

not until today did i know
that you have amphibian genes—
look, under your reddish green
your webbed hands cling
to the concrete— my dear 蔦ivy

石壁に這いて色づく蔦の葉のかわずのごとき指渇きおり

Time in Britain　— a land nine hours behind you —

1

one second before two
the short hand retreats
thirty degrees again —
now my watch as well
enters 冬the winter season

午後二時の一秒前に一時へと戻りスマホは冬を始める

2

loneliness for 刹那a moment
when crossing the line
of three p.m.—at home you become
a dweller of tomorrow, leaving me
    behind

十五時を過ぎる刹那のさびしさよ日本が先に明日となりて

I Love You

frog-handed ivy and question-mark-tail squirrel
one-hour leap at night in October and in March
stubborn limescale in the electric kettle
a bathroom without a bath but a toilet bowl
staff members and professors addressed by their first names
ramen that should not be called by the name ramen
realising centred behaviour with red wavy lines
second floor called first and first floor called ground

I love you
all the more for them

LUCY CUNDILL

Lucy Cundill is a poet whose poems so reflect her own lived experience that anything she could write here would be redundant. Her work has been published, and will continue to be published, whether you like it or not. She lives in Norwich. Her work has been described as containing "a lot of screaming".

lcundill7@gmail.com
@futile.devicez on Instagram

Funny How Things Turn Out

you are 20 years old
that is both a **big** and a ~~small~~
number / it is ~~small~~ in the fact that
the door-to-door salesman still asks
if mum or dad is in / it is **big**
in the fact that they are not / this is ~~your house~~
your landlord's house / it is December
22nd / you are 20 years old and
this is the 1st Christmas you're going to spend
alone / that is both related and ~~unrelated~~
to the pandemic / it is ~~unrelated~~ in the fact that
you have been waiting / your whole life
to get away / it is related in the fact that
you were going to do Christmas on the 26th
with your boyfriend who you love like death but
you probably have the virus from a friend
who you shared a joint with / the cheek of it
as well it was your weed but that's what
friends are for / giving you potentially life-threatening
diseases = making you sick in repayment for all the
so-many times they made you well / it's okay
you are twenty years old that is **exactly** the right
kind of number to be in this situation to avoid
complications / a non-lethal number it's funny how
you always want to leave until | **death's standing there holding
his front door open** | and then
youtakeitallbackyoutake***everything***/youare sitting
in the fire escape of the attic room of the housemate you like
the least / you think this would be a beautiful place
to smoke weed / you haven't smoked in 48 hours now
that is both a **big** and a small number it is **big**
in the fact that you're ~~kind of~~ addicted / well ~~not~~
"addicted" just *"reluctant to quit"* / it's a family thing
it is small in the fact it was easier / than you expected
to become like everyone else / the problem is
we always promise ourselves that we wouldn't ever be like them
but never think to promise ourselves that we wouldn't ever ***love***
somebody like them / in your brain's blind-spot
it's ridiculously easy to love / someone who was made

the same as those who you were taught to love
growing up and easily enough / it becomes a prerequisite but
it goes both ways like everything does / he is <u>both</u>
the person you <u>don't</u> want to love but do / just
as / you are the person he <u>doesn't</u> want to love but does
at least neither of you are the person you do want to love but <u>don't</u>
that's for later / that's an entirely different kind of problem

Everything Contains You

▶ I find myself looking at

fractured images of a life once lived ❚ ❚ ▶ this is the instead life

the instead life hurts better

feelsbettertastesbetterfucksbetterlovesbetterkillsyouquicker

and then slower

again ❚ ❚ ▶ a heart never finds out

what does it want ❚ ❚

▶ why does it ache ❚ ❚ ▶ ache is a complicated word

like child love regret ❚ ❚ ▶ these words turn into weapons

loaded with complicated meanings ❚ ❚ ▶ complicated meanings kill conversations and

❚ ❚

▶ create complicated ones ❚ ❚ ▶ you complicate my contemplation

looking at fractured images of a life once lived

loved fuckedforgottenbroughtbackfromthedeadresuscitatedagain

and again and again ❚ ❚ ▶ I love you

again◀

◀ and again◀

◀ and again◀◀ I find myself looking at

fractured images of a life once lived ◀◀

again◀◀ and again◀◀ and again◀◀

▶again▶▶ and again▶▶ and again▶▶

fractured images of a life once lived ▶▶

and again▶▶ I find myself looking at

again▶

▶ and again▶

and again and again ❚ ❚ ▶ I love

looking at fractured images of a life once lived

loved fuckedforgottenbroughtbackfromthedeadresuscitatedagain

▶ I create complicated ones ▌▐ ▶ you complicate my contemplation

loaded with complicated meanings ▌▐ ▶ complicated meanings kill conversations

and ▌▐

▶ like child love regret ▌▐ ▶ these words turn into weapons

why does it ache ▌▐ ▶ ache is a complicated word

what does it want

again ▌▐ ▶ a heart never finds out

and then slower

feels...better...tastes...better...fucks...better...loves...better...kills...you...quicker

the instead life hurts better ■■■■■■■■■■■■■■■■■■■■■■■■

fractured images of a life once lived ▌▐ ▶ this is the instead life

I find myself looking at ■

Rationalise This.

Asking whether the glass is half full
or half empty is the man's way
of asking if the girl drowning inside it
is okay. Either way, he has completely neglected its contents.
I told him I would rather drown in love than in hate. He said, well actually,
drowning's the same, either way.

He then asked me what I wanted. I said I wanted to be more
than just a sexually appealing afterthought in a man's mind's eye. He laughed
and then I woke up and realised I was a woman.

Being a woman is a lot like being a poet
in that no one is actually interested in anything you have to say.
For instance, I might be at the top of my voice screaming
I AM STANDING ON A PRECIPICE AND NOT LOOKING DOWN
and they'd say, go on, son.

In The Womb of a Horse

I identify as a feminist
          in the same way man
          identifies as an animal.
He doesn't   but he is one   <u>whether he likes it or not.</u>

I identify as a woman
          in the same way man
          identifies as an animal.
          He knows he is but he tries   <u>to erase it from himself.</u>

I identify as queer
          in the same way man
          identifies as an animal.
He would   speak about it more   <u>if people let him.</u>

    I identify as a poet
          more than I identify
          with anything else.
This poem does not <u>identify as a metaphor.</u>

                                          <u>This poem identifies</u>
                                          as a trojan horse.

Spoilers For Loving Men

Mercury burned cold one night. You shot and killed the stag of your sense
so he could eat, and his children could grow. You lived in the bodies
of people who didn't look like you, not even the mirror could diagnose a self.
You repeated their stories, worries, and dreams,
until you couldn't remember your own. Mother was right when she said,
the hypnotist won't sell you happiness, but he will buy your soul.

Somewhere out there, you're drowning in the lake and he's
stationed by the shore. At the table, on TV, they tell the story
of how he would have been able to save you, if only you'd
appeared to him at the right time, in the right place, if only you'd tried at all.
Alone, he dreams of the son he once was, and tries to piece together
a caricature of being whole. Only under his breath does he mutter
how he would have loved to destroy you, if only he could have got there first.

What becomes of you then? Do you die wrapped in cloth
or do you dream of dust, do you eat your hate in the hopes of keeping him safe
    from it,
uncaring of what it might cost, do you sing the childhood hymns he had almost
    forgot,
in the hope that someday, somebody might change the words? No.
Remember the sins and the stories of the footprints, and holes punched
in the wall, that adorn the path to your bedroom door. The only way to save
    yourself
from what has been foretold
would be to become unlovable,
or in other words, to ensure that yourself is only yours.

Things I Sometimes Miss

- → the love I lost to a man who hadn't yet discovered the meaning of the word ;
- → the entire county of Norfolk ;
- → a terraced house duplicated a thousand times over ;
- → a box room full of people older than me ;
- → drugs, for the first time ;
- → love, for the first time ;
- → a cigarette, and every cigarette after ;
- → pesto pasta before it became disgusting ;
- → acquaintances I loved like family ;
- → the latest nights with everyone in surround sound, screaming the words ;
- → smoking hash with your best friend on a balcony in London ;
- → a shed and a circle of friends ;
- → a flat and a lover ;
- → the best cat in the world buried in a garden in Brundall ;
- → a party, and of course vomit ;
- → vanilla vodka, diet coke ;
- → kebab shop cheesy chips ;
- → the feeling of taking off barefoot down the street from a party ;
- → being able to get so drunk you don't feel anything ;
- → a long chain of things precariously restraining the original problem

NAOISE GALE

Naoise Gale is a poet from Huddersfield. Her debut pamphlet *After the Flood Comes the Apologies* is out with Nine Pens Press and won 3rd prize in the Poetry Book Awards. She was the winner of the Ledbury Poetry Competition 2022, and more recently, her work has been published in Lighthouse Journal, Tears in the Fence, and Atrium.

Contact email: Naoisegale@gmail.com
Social media: @Naoisegale13 on Twitter
Website: https://linktr.ee/naoisegale

6th August

It starts like this: an argument unremembered.
The Girl who is almost a woman in the womb-dark

piercing her skin with silver. Shrieking
like a midnight kettle. Un-boning her body to

cotton and water. The records say she was
"alone in her room" which means after a glut

of threats, popped pyrotechnics, she did it.
Which means she couldn't remember why

she died, although the how was her mother's
bread torn apart by fingers and a hasty

harvest of pharmaceuticals, but she died nonetheless
and fifteen minutes later was curled like a cord

around her mother, who was mopping her face
with a cold compress, holding her hand and

watching phone footage of rock concerts loud
as blood and bone. There was a lull in the room

like the ghosts had gorged on milk
and in their fat suits were indulging in naptime.

There was a heat too, skin gripping innards
hot as a fridge's arse and burst-vessel red.

The noticing equalled time speeding up, until
everything happened in a hurry and a slice of malt loaf

and a carrier bag for vomit and the sort of magic and urgency
only practiced by witches and mothers.

Who promise not to ask questions. Who bundle
their children into cars like bin-bags full of shit clothes

for the charity-shop, teal sequinned dresses two sizes
too small from when twelve years old and bad taste.

Who drape wet fabric when the heat becomes an undeniable
itch, when the remorse is swallowed by nausea.

Who open all the windows just to keep you safe.

Birmingham New Street

Twenty minute dissociative
journey stain
for rockabye lady with TikTok tunes
and no jacket. Five-pound ticket,
idyllic, always costs the same.
Plaits unravel

to parcel tape. Skirt grips knickers, tights tear
as predicted. Impulsive self-care/ self-
harm at crazy miles per hour. If it's dark
on arrival, are you sectionable?
Good girl junkies go pharmacy

to pharmacy, smile like pale
suns, all white teeth and cheeks.
The station chemist never
puts out — flirting is mere interrogation:

Are these for yourself? May I ask
how old you are? Are you on
any other medication?
Have you taken it before?
What's this for? My colleague
says she saw you last week —
sorry, we have to check. Maybe talk
to your doctor. This might make you sleepy,
so no driving or operating
heavy machinery.
You're very young,
what hurts so bad?

[YES SIR. NO SIR. CAN'T DRIVE SIR. DON'T KNOW SIR.]

Nights get long this time of year.
Public transport leaky and absent,
our new mother. Cold angry fuck-off passengers
plot one-nighters with the dry mild,
armouring themselves

with newspapers and brown bags
and high street carriers and film-thin coats.
Boxes of schokokuss mallows propped
under elbows, gift wrap long as rifles,

singing plastic pets kennelled in cardboard, new
dresses (all sequins), ulcer-red lipstick. Pills
get hard to hoard: Black Friday; relatives; strange hours;
childhood bedrooms; strapped for cash; limited

secrecy. Success is a quick smiling script,
mossy coppers, no receipt. Wet numb stroll
through the Bullring, craving salt. Hour and a half
in the dark cold, beaten by bags, rubber soles split
from bridge to heel, socks sodden, blisters baubling

on new, shining skin. Wind through tunnels
like a bell. Nostalgia for something not yet
experienced. Quivering, desperate pill.

as it wasn't

the nurses fluttered between
bedsides arms soft and wide
as downy pillows the doctors
had rabbit faces and pocket mints
and empathetic yarns twirling
from their listening mouths
the floors glinted an egg-speckled
white everything was shiny
as a brash mausoleum everything
was peaceful as a brush-stroke
we were singing to each other
to spindle out the morphine
we knew we would wake up
tomorrow smiling.

DANIEL NORTHOVER

Daniel Northover is a poet, musician and text-based artist living in the south of England. His work explores experiences of contemplation, emptiness, and healing. He waters his cactus once a month with just a teaspoon of water. He can be found on Instagram @_daniel_northover_.

drlnorthover@gmail.com

the beach

     planets – toning the
    sheets under the world
   with their grace – with
  walking – just as the sun
 does – in flirting with the world
tap dancing under hot
blue sky

sternum stars burst
 trickling down the fabric
  of –
    sitting there – dressing
    cosmos taking it
     all mine – all in

     hopefully foam – like bed
      dressing sand in warmth and
      falling – will i disappear

     groaning – so
      the midnight – shore steps
     on my room –

hurt on my chest
 i – if it is i –
  curling on shore
  i am still there –
  sand passes

    *

    tracking pain up
    from breath – where it goes
     i – if it is i – contain all this
    blue – keeping said words
   on this – beyond it is
  so blue today

humming on roads where
   tar lays – heating into
sinking miles above core

   curling feet – bare on
      heat – this surface where heads thump
         beating correct rhythm and proportion
            enough to hush – left to right of cars

      so persisting – in the dark of
         several moments kept – in hurt
            i – if it is i – will not let up
            i will wreck your mind

      i am all good – coming from nothing
         pointing to chest
      deep under living ocean – it's everywhere
   which in this other world – clean as
   shedded snakes – left its skin to
us – drowning in this new water light
so generous – where all the good comes from

i'll heartstorm the words

   chest plates easing
   open – light finally
   besides – gushing cars
   –
so weary
of
   emptiness

highway poem for jonas mekas

i lived eternal
without experience – i came
into boundless rooms – with no
access to things – bones were bones

compassion had it's name and it's fruits
were rich but i had yet to recognise
the taste – i lived without trees – i lived in
shallow breath – the world had little colour and i
glistened like marble
in hope – not yet bashed but
dying in my own time

years on
jet black ground
hot with efforts of
drivers – of night travels into
towns where friends are poured
and bruises remain to be made in
fights and communion with
stars – only noticed in the upward stare on the final steps
home

the highway had yet to be
walked all the way home by anyone
it had past it's time – sealed off invisible
lights stood tall and rested
gazing upon us – light smiles
cats eyes

sunken poles
nothing bothering them
behind – masses of
trees – hazy from night

i loved them so much
metal and rust sewed behind
vision – glued skies
heaving woods – tiny swaying

names dropped off
the world – objects made
of music

jonas mekas and his films
made sense from then on

excerpt from *jackal*

jackal rose
today from peculiar sleep
jackal dreamt of a wise elder
guide coyote who once held jackal
through a storm / returned following years of
independence for one more hunt of the mind / the moment
jackal passed through the gateless plain / which was not the same
space / jackal's vision shook and the thorns in jackal's brain went away
and jackal broke down in gleeful tears / melting the weight of neuroses off a
tired back not because there had been recent suffering but in this great cave we can
be honest / and only here could jackal once weep / jackal has been stuffed by
all the help received / jackal does not go to sleep in a cage nor disappear /
jackal and the I learn to love one another / though the one by the river
jackal now knows is real / the hot sand on feet melted in the cosmic
blood / rain by the crimson sky / bleeding cliffs surround jackal
by the shore / up on the hot sandy hill a cave was
beginning on the way jackal comes to the black
hole in the sand / void of heat and smell of
stones / descending / before it is too late
coming to where it is only love
it is there in that space that
jackal rose

EMMA BROWN

Emma Brown grew up in Shropshire, lives in London and was a Development Executive before taking her MA. Inspired by her background in film and television her poetry is cinematic with a focus on capturing fleeting moments and ideas. She has been published in *aswirl* and *Sentire*.

emabrown@hotmail.co.uk

You live in Sussex – I Googled it

I can't stop loving you Ray Mears
your boots caked in mud and your craggy adventures

Show me how to light a fire
using only an apple core and a kind word

You build me a shelter
to keep out split clouds and boredom

You lend me a green shirt with pockets full of useful things
a joke, a knife, confidence, a medieval feast

served on a banquet table made out of a tree
you felled with the power of your mind

When we met in London
 it was just like a romcom

I had lost my map
you showed me the way to Rupert Street

where we shared a pina colada
and a profound belief in time travel

It's hard to share you with the telly and your fans
but you clinch it by inviting me on a trip to Nemo's Point

You tell me to pack a good book,
some salt and the element of surprise

We end up in a lifeboat, clinging together
sole survivors of an orca attack

fathoms high above the seabed
lying side by side on a bright orange raft

Now it's just us
uninterrupted

pushed and pulled by the moon
thousands of miles from land

thinking of all the ways
to never get rescued

Inspired by - I Can't Stop Loving You John Keats by Kim Addonizio

I am the snow

dressed all in white
I surprise-visit you
with a midwinter flurry

I stride across the land
drape my full-moon white scarf
along your roads

shrug off my overcoat
to mute your rooves and hilltops
in mistletoe-berry white

I semaphore *we are so far from the sun*
with my white-flag white handkerchiefs
that fall on fields and lakes

As I drift through counties
I collect time like discarded treasure
kept safe in my glacial pockets

I rest on the white-cliff white coast
dissect the hours and minutes
into seconds

examine them
as snowflakes under a microscope
complicated and temporary

In a world I've made quiet for you
I wait for the tilt
back towards the light and longer days

The chef demonstrates

He slices life out of the eel
with a deep cut to the back of the head

nails it through the gill-slit
to the chopping board

He runs his fingers and knife along the spine
opens the long body like a book

white flesh hinged by bloodied bone
guts out, fillets carved

the dorsal fin
and the memory of swimming

are tossed in the bin
with teeth, scales and eyes

all that is left is the heart
held in the palm of his hand

still beating
glossy red cells, the size of a hazelnut

clench
and release

clench
and release

It can last for hours
He says

She recognises the horror
and magic of this electrical cascade

senses the pulse and currents
that move

the wet jelly
of her brain

without applause
the chef wipes his blade clean

FLORA BEAGLEY

Flora Beagley is based between London and East Anglia. Her work lives in the interwoven greyness of poetry and prose, where she finds merging the two unbinding. Her writing explores time, Anglo-Finnish heritage, bodies and memory. This year she was shortlisted for the *Driftwood Press* prize. She works at the Royal Academy of Arts.

Florabeagle6@gmail.com

Sutton Hoo

All our lives we have swum the flatland's wæter
east-west; swuster, swuster, bróþor, bróþor.
We are four fisc from guð
knows where says mum and I stroke the bones
that we share. Two of us have the same thigh,
the other two the same hair. I do not know if they brought us
here by boat and I do not know if I care. A great cyning
is buried here. I fear I think things small
because my hands can get to them; a rib cage
imprint and a gilded lyre.

I turn my face for the photo
and I know that we can smell
each other's scalps. With love,
I think of how smells die. Cyning,
did you share a scalp
with your sibling, did you share
a thigh?

swuster, swuster, bróþor, bróþor

There isn't a word for that.

Study of a sculpture

What a hole
 thigh is. Everyday
  she changes colour; ink smudged
  tin green, cast
   green, seaweed
    with a lick of paint? She carves
     it is okay to not know what you are
    and we spit
    and mourn leg
    or latch onto this most. Her port
   hole is a bending elbow
   or field's window. She makes shapes
   something. Make sure the weather
  merely colours her skin. No plinth
 for constant clamber
within.

Renaissance

I have seen it done, this writhing. All the times I do
and the times before, in those paintings and films
of Italian men beating blood out of each other's
mouths. I confess I thought it meant the brink
of life so death; that the body nested itself in violent
clamming. But then when it came to me it cruelled
my skin and changed where I thought organs
lived. It pumped me with things like rain — I tied
my knot to the belly of the shore for days.

I hate to say I never felt more alive.

fáinne Chladaigh

Celtic knots lured the devil to unsolvable patterns; trapping them in a never ending loop, they were prevented from ever passing through to the knot's creator.

Opulled
same. Your hand is drawn to drawing
the knot cold on my neck. This is my chosen
masonry — yours, finger bare
except for the ring; hands winged, heart
crowned. I do not know if it is up or down, right
or wrong, upside down. I know I am lying
around you. My necklace spills
from body to bed — it too lies
on the feather plinth. Something has sucked
you into an unhappening: a square
circle, grip melted, something frozen infinite
in loop. You knot. No devil
has ever passed through you yet
now, you do not give yourself
over. Handle me
through my jewellery.

You move your mouth as if to speak.

No knot unfurls, your voice
too weak. Here

Milk bottle

Something
has gone to seed,
so now it must become a story. Maybe
you are not ready for it: lip-curled and birthed
on the table. Foiled and fat as it is. Sit - I'll unfurl you

some glug.

Dandelions

When I was young, I did not know they were the same — the yellow dandelion and feathered, splayed same as cotton, the ones you can blow and baste

breath with wish. Pins lining the breeze. Is that stupid?

Years ago, hands sticky, I plucked rooted stem from soil. The organs of a weed scraggled and limped in the air. The soil was crumbling velvet. I held my breath, took the tip of my hand and balded the head of seeds. They felt soft as a scalp.

My hands felt bloodied for hours.

I still do not know which comes first. Perhaps it ends life a seedling; soft-haired, child

bending its stem and O-ing

a spitted wish.

Wishes can be made with weeds. Weeds, stone and tin.

MISHAL AHMAD

Mishal is an aspiring female poet from Pakistan. Her work explores themes of guilt, retribution, spirituality, introspection, death wish, juxtaposing ideas of free will and fate mostly as a gothic fever dream.

Contact email: mishal.ahmad217@gmail.com
Instagram: mishal.mg.mg
sqe23mbu@uea.ac.uk

They Told Us To Take Our Mind Off Morbid Decaying Things

A leopard rapidly repairs itself settles into a new life

Suicides glittering with self reflection
But how long will we carry a death wish

A leopard is   infrequent   near
     afar   elusive
       inviolable

     tranquil
A leopard is   mirth
sometimes disastrous   unacknowledged   unsung

the song of the soul

But a leopard can't be denied

Listen listen to what it says!

A Leopard is kin

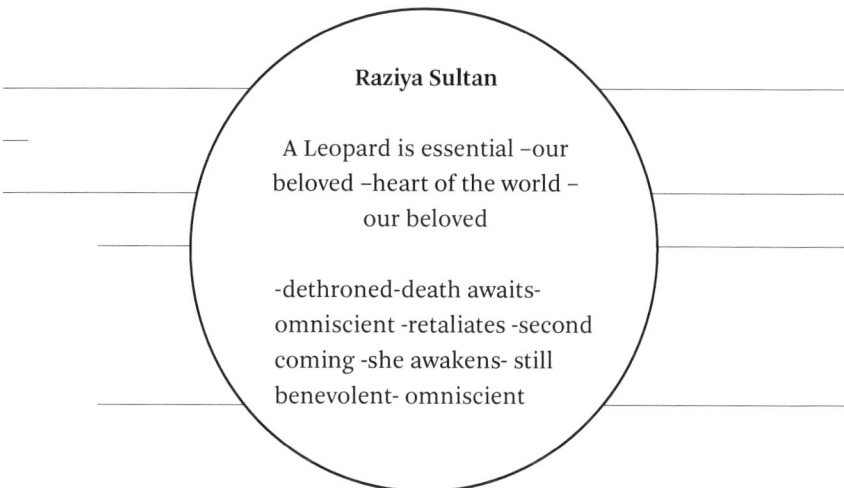

Raziya Sultan

A Leopard is essential –our beloved –heart of the world – our beloved

-dethroned-death awaits- omniscient -retaliates -second coming -she awakens- still benevolent- omniscient

We Loved The Stars And Then Moved On

We are not for this world
Overtaken by cessation
In aversion

Nicotine again
After life you live in me-suicides spaced-no sign of life -lion after line -you live in us now-line every line-cathartic stages of silent screams -hope this guilt stays with us - suicides spaced -mutinously staged -the in-between secrecy and silence- suicides staged – resident rebel here-suicides delayed --no pattern - no pattern none -suicides spaced - silent study-goes unnoticed

Nothing And Then Finally A Newfound Monarch To Whisper about

from a futile incision an insect of form still void of content / a mirror tied to the eyelid / a disclosure finally furnishes this heart/we've clumsily used up all our wishes to see ufos in our cities for the macabre has lost all its appeal/we still keep the skull but the macabre has lost its comfort/so here it is a delayed insect of discarded accusations and cautious confessions/no we won't be at ease until we decay and stay forgotten /till we have a plant a rock a bird a horse wild horse the turin horse / a dog /your dog your dog is now our dog /your dog is now our dog you can keep your cat /we want to kill all men and just your dog / a man his faltering myth his fragile divinity / we liked him enough to let him live/these expiring deities / always an indifferent god forever our muse / a monotheist/a monotheist for melpomene/ a monotheist for marx /a maggot /the mighty maggot monarch we let it eat/ eat the czar, eat churchill enjoy it keep eating churchill / eat the warmongers eat all presidents /even eat rasputin /an assonance a resonance/ a bulge a creak a spill /bring the quill / some insipid twist/we've pledged our fidelity to everyday occurrences to the magic of the mundane / we hate that you love us and nothing excites us more than betraying your trust

A Graffiti Artist Time Travels Endlessly Effortlessly But Doesn't List It On Their CV

Transience

The smell of pain each time we time travel
Transience is a zealot's phlegm a believer's atonement
Transience is a salvager's omniscient offering
How long will we protect our fates and for what ?
Transience is the resultant pathos from a shrinking time an outlived memory
Why we can't give up why we try to occupy each moment
Transience is this reckless moment's careful   alibi
Transience is that exonerated moment's overtures to restoration
How long will we protect our fates and for whom ?
Transience is the vestige of our self control
Why we are so careful about negating the power of renunciation
The vantage point for all our foredoomed misguided transgressions
Why we let things unfold the way they do
Yet time still hunts us down
Why we can't coexist or mirror each other
Why our self-control ends and the gods begin
Death
Why the gods design our fates with no remorse
And yet we remain steadfast believers in a better world
Despite never being cleared of relishing the roles we were doomed to play eagerly occupying the same fate over and over again

Our Happily, Ever After Getting Too Repetitive

Death
We always liked the way death
tracks us lands amidst
us
our adamant scaffold our
sustained continuous
scaffold
 we love the way death
shows us a way out each
time equalizes us all
 our gentlest scaffold our
kindest scaffold

a leviathan relents
Encased within the tableau of a faithless life that
so rife with prostrations to an evasive leviathan
was
    atlas of mass solar suicides
an unceaseless sea of stale prayers frothing away
in dormancy of a nonbeliever's firm hold
    atlas adored adorned reprinted republished
    redrawn
Vent out it must a pestilence but it's all man
made

our fury, our own locally curated man made
pestilence of choice
    atlas repeated redrawn
as long you grant us a recurring death wish we'll
live happily ever after
    we stopped trying
    seeking comfort in continuity
  relentless ambiguity when it's all about her
    all else is the loudest silence
    atlas relinquished
    We stand exalted !
    All else goes in a requiem

To Be Continued

exiting Eden/ with a respiring supplication/ perished ruling class

/ brand new self-reliant martyred comrades and a resorted Elysium

InshaAllah, the soldiers will retreat

and the dead will finally cease to exist

ACKNOWLEDGEMENTS

Literary Translation

We firstly owe huge thanks to our brilliant course tutors – Cecilia Rossi, Tom Boll and Duncan Large – without whose guidance and wisdom, our time on this MA would surely not have been as formative, our classes as engaging, nor our memories as fond. More than anything, we've had the chance to learn and experience the joy of translating, and it is a joy we will most definitely take with us.

Many thanks to all those talented translators (and to a certain talented musician) who took the time and care to prepare and deliver such intellectually stimulating workshops and seminars. These sessions, led by Jean Boase-Beier, Sawad Hussain, Don Bartlett, Sophie Stevens, Nariman Youssef, Michele Hutchison, Sasja Janssen, Denise Kripper, Kari Dickson and Haftor Medbøe, have helped shape both our practice and understanding of translation.

We would also like to extend our gratitude to Anna Goode and the BCLT team, as well as Helen Busby at the Archive, who, in offering us countless enriching opportunities whilst fostering a supportive and welcoming environment here at UEA, have helped make our experience an overwhelmingly positive one.

And last, but certainly not least, we are immensely grateful to the 2023/24 MA Literary Translation cohort – part-timers included. As Ceci has often said, this group is our first network of translators, and we can't think of a more supportive, collaborative and inspiring group of creatives to begin this journey with. From the lively and insightful debates in seminars (occasionally interrupted by an appearance from our honorary Feline>English translator Sylvester), to custom-made memes in the group chat to keep us all laughing through summative season, we are incredibly lucky to have been brought together in this lovely little corner of the literary world. Through this course we have learnt that translation is anything but a solitary endeavour and we very much look forward to keeping in touch, sharing ideas and reading each other for many years to come.

Eileen Craigie, Megan Harvey, Jon Herring, Paris Jonchier-Litwack, Caitlin McKie and Chris Salpingidis

Poetry

This anthology is a collection, and celebration, of the work written by the cohort of poets who took part in UEA's 2023–24's Creative Writing MA: Poetry.

We'd like to thank our tutors, Tiffany Atkinson, Holly Corfield-Carr, Jos Smith and Andrea Holland. Your enthusiasm and patience has helped push ourselves and our poetry beyond where we were when we began back in September 2023. Thank you for believing in us and making us better poets.

We'd like to also thank the various other members of the Literature, Drama and Creative Writing department. There are too many to name, but you have undoubtedly added to the atmosphere here at UEA which unshackles us poets. A special thank you goes to the poets who have come and spoken or performed to us at UEA, your words were inspiring and comforting.

To the city of Norwich, we thank you for making us feel welcome to live and experiment here. For some of us it wasn't a far journey. For others it was the opposite side of the country or even the opposite side of the world. The city's universal enthusiasm for literature has made it easier for us to belong here. We'd like to especially thank the organisations, UEA Live, TOAST Poetry, Poets in the Cellar and Last Poet Standing for giving us platforms to perform and practice voicing our poetry publicly.

Thank you to our fellow coursemates. Sharing work, especially in its earliest forms, can be a vulnerable experience but each of you have made this a safe space to express our work. It has been a delight as well as inspirational to respond to so many unique and talented poets. Your comments have helped produce many more lines which wouldn't have been written.

A final thank you to our friends and family – you are our rocks.

Written by Michael Athey on behalf of the Poetry Anthology Editors (Michael Athey, Dana Collins, Meier Smith, Lucy Cundill, Mishal Ahmad, Daniel Northover).

UEA MA Creative Writing Anthologies: Poetry and Translated Literature

First published by Egg Box Publishing, 2024
Part of the UEA Publishing Project Ltd.

International © retained by individual authors

This book is sold subject to the condition that it shall not, by way of trade or otherwise, be lent, resold, hired out, stored in a retrieval system, or otherwise circulated without the publisher's prior consent in any form of binding or cover other than that in which it is published and without a similar condition including this condition being imposed on the subsequent purchaser.

A CIP record for this book is available from the British Library
Printed and bound in the UK by Imprint Digital

Designed by Emily Benton Book Design
emilybentonbookdesign.co.uk

Distributed by BookSource
50 Cambuslang Road
Cambuslang
Glasgow
G32 8NB
+44 (0)141 642 9192
booksource.net

ISBN 978-1-915812-61-2